MR SMITH'S
INDOOR GARDEN

by Geoffrey Smith

Illustrated by Maggie Raynor
Edited by Brian Davies

BRITISH BROADCASTING CORPORATION

Published to accompany the BBC-tv series *Mr Smith's Indoor Garden* produced by Brian Davies and first broadcast on BBC-2 on Wednesdays from January–March 1980.

Published to accompany a series of programmes prepared in consultation with the BBC Continuing Education Council.

Other BBC books by the author

Mr Smith's Gardening Book
Mr Smith's Vegetable Garden
Mr Smith's Flower Garden
Mr Smith's Fruit Garden
Mr Smith Propagates Plants

The photographs on front and back covers and page 4 were specially taken by Cavendish Studios

First published 1979. Reprinted 1980
Published by the British Broadcasting Corporation
35 Marylebone High Street, London W1M 4AA

Photoset in 9/10 Plantin VIP by Northampton Phototypesetters Ltd
and printed in England by
Belmont Press Ltd, Northampton

ISBN: 0 563 16313 5

Contents

Introduction

My apprenticeship to gardening was served in a large private garden and, in addition to looking after acres of lawns, borders, and greenhouses, there were great banks of pot plants in the house to be taken care of by the gardening staff.

I can remember my introduction to indoor gardening vividly when at 7 a.m. one Monday morning a watering can was pushed into my hands with the terse instruction 'See to the plants in THE HOUSE'. The head gardener took a great pride in the quality of the plants used to decorate the main hall, staircase, dining room etc., and I was under no illusion as to my fate if anything went wrong. Never have plants been subject to such individual attention, but even in the midst of anxiety I could not help but be impressed at how foliage and flowers brought life and beauty to the rooms. I still think that a room without plants, no matter how expensively furnished, lacks both interest and warmth.

Geoffrey Smith

Preface

Growing plants indoors is a hobby which anyone with the slightest interest in gardening can enjoy. Indeed, there are positive advantages: no fears of May frost or July gales disturb the tranquil ordered progress of the indoor gardener. Today, when so many people live in flats the cultivation of house plants becomes even more important, filling an instinctive need and beautifying the home at the same time.

Indoor plants fall into well defined groups, the true house plant which can be grown permanently in a room usually has decorative foliage with the flowers, if any, merely a seasonal bonus. The other main group is the flowering or florists pot plants which are treated as temporary decoration. Bulbs fall into this category, as do Cyclamen, Cineraria, and Poinsettia. Whether genuine house plants or the temporary florist varieties, each requires skill in cultivation and provides the same satisfaction that is to be derived from a well kept garden outdoors. No matter which direction your gardening interests take, make sure that before buying any plant you can provide the right conditions to make growing it a possibility rather than an outside chance.

Take time over choosing plants, even one of the easy to grow range, particularly if it is being added to an established collection. Check the foliage carefully to make sure you are not buying trouble in the shape of pests or disease. Greenfly, whitefly and scale insects can hide on a leaf, or under a leaf and then infect all the plants in the room. Specialist plants are best bought from a nursery, garden centre or shop where the people in charge know enough to look after them properly. All but the most resilient house plants will suffer severely if exposed for sale on an open stall in the market or on a shelf in a multiple store for a long time.

Ask for advice when buying – what compost is it grown in? essential information when the time comes to re-pot. What temperature would be suitable? How often will feeding and watering be necessary?

Reject plants grown in dirty slimy compost or with a mass of roots pushing through the drainage hole. One indicates careless watering or feeding, the other that the roots are badly pot bound. Both could lessen your chances of keeping the plant alive.

The greatest single influence over the plants chosen is what sort of conditions the various rooms in the house offer. Within this limitation you can give free rein to personal choice. Grouping plants together which need similar temperatures, watering and feeding, makes them that much easier to look after.

Growing Conditions

Temperature and Humidity

Though many house plants will put up with considerable fluctuations in temperature, a too rapid and frequent variation will do damage. Many house plants will withstand quite cool temperatures providing these are constant or the change in climate is gradual.

The majority of house plants are damaged if grown in a very dry atmosphere. The leaves lose moisture so quickly the roots cannot replace it, even though well supplied with water. Unfortunately, the air in a centrally heated house is usually very dry. Standing the pots in a tray of moist gravel (1), or plunging them in a container filled with moist peat (2) or damp newspaper will improve the humidity. As the material dries it maintains a layer of clammy air around the leaves. Spraying the foliage every day with water will also help. The pint sized container sold for applying pesticides is ideal for providing the fine mist of water which helps the plants without ruining the furniture.

Draughts are as objectionable to plants as they are to human beings, so avoid places near doors which open directly outside. Extremes of heat are just as injurious. Positions near an open fire, alongside a radiator or on top of a television set will soon cause browning of the foliage. Moist heat is a different matter; plants like the Saintpaulia (African Violets) thrive on a bathroom windowsill.

There is little point in spending time and effort in cultivating a plant with beautiful foliage if the colour is marred by a coating of grime. The leaves are covered with tiny holes, and it is through these that the plant takes in air, passes out waste gases, and evaporates surplus moisture. Dust clogs up these holes, reducing their efficiency, so cleaning the leaves makes them more attractive and improves their function. A wipe with a moist soft cloth or cotton wool once a week (3) is all that is required. Alternatively, special products can be bought which after application put a gloss on the leaves while at the same time removing the dust.

Always, when trying one of the leaf cleaning chemicals for the first time, check that it will not harm the plant. I have a routine which, to date, has saved me making several catastrophic blunders. I use a sponge dipped in luke warm water to free the leaves from grime, then at intervals the leaves are treated with one of the special cleaning products which has first been given a thorough trial on one leaf only of a selection of plants. If that leaf is not harmed it can safely be used on the whole plant EXCEPT the young leaves. NEVER HANDLE YOUNG LEAVES or use a cleaner on them.

Light

No plants, not even ferns, so popular in Victorian houses, will grow in deep shade. Most prefer good diffused daylight with shade from direct sunlight, particularly at mid-day during summer time. There are plants which can accommodate bright sunlight, just as there are those which will adjust to quite shady conditions in a north facing room, but the majority grow best in good but diffused light. Dark corners can be improved by fitting special lighting, but the normal house lights are not usually bright enough to recompense for the absence of natural light. Rooms with only very small windows will be unsuitable for growing anything but the hardiest of house plants.

Feeding

Feeding is adjusted according to need, taking into consideration the time of year, vigour of growth, and whether the plant has recently been re-potted. When a plant is dormant it will not need feeding. On the other hand, in the full vigour of growth a heavy foliaged plant may need feeding every 14 days. After re-potting no extra fertilizer will be needed for three months or even longer. What type of feed is used, provided it is specially formulated for indoor plants, depends on personal choice or availability. Single action fertilizers as opposed to mixtures are used only to correct an obvious deficiency. For example, the yellowing of the leaves on Citrus mitis which indicates a lack of magnesium can be corrected by watering with a pinch of Epsom salts dissolved in a pint of water. Otherwise, mixtures containing a proper balance of nitrogen, phosphates and potash, either in liquid, powder, or tablet form will supply all the food required. Whatever the fertilizer chosen there are two golden rules to observe before applying it. First, READ the instructions on the packet carefully, and DO NOT add just that little bit extra above the recommended dose – it will do more harm than good. Excess fertilizer soon sours a compost, and in some cases will actually kill the plants' roots. In fact, overfeeding of house plants will do almost the same amount of damage as starving them of nutrients. A mass of foliage which is soft and too large indicates excess, whereas hard, stunted growth means the roots are starved. Never feed a sickly plant i.e. one where the foliage is going brown or yellow or wilting. Sick plants like sick human beings need to have the cause of illness diagnosed, and then treated. Check for overwatering, or dryness at the root or in the atmosphere. Make sure there are no draughts or fumes, and finally see that the roots are not pot-bound.

Watering

Probably the chief failure to grow any plant successfully indoors is overwatering. Excessive concern with watering by keeping the compost saturated all the time, even during the resting period, is an act of kindness which kills. Sodden compost becomes sour, increasingly acid, and totally deprived of oxygen. Under these conditions plant roots die through lack of air, and fungi attack the stem at soil level. Constant watering washes out plant foods which, unless replaced, results in starvation.

No set rules can be laid down as to how often a plant needs water; this depends entirely on the type of compost, temperature of the room, and whether it is in active growth or enjoying a rest. Some plants, in any case, need more moisture than others. 'Mother-in-Law's Tongue' will survive a drought better than a 'Busy Lizzie' because it is adapted to growing in desert regions. To check if a plant needs a drink, scratch the surface of the compost (1) – if it is moist a quarter to half an inch down then do not water. Conversely, if the soil is dry then plunge the pot to half its depth in a bowl containing rainwater or tepid mains water and leave until the moisture rises to the surface of the compost (2). Plants such as Azaleas which are killed by lime can be watered with clean rainwater, or water collected when de-frosting the 'fridge'. The alternative, of applying water to the top of the pot until it runs out at the bottom is not one which I recommend. In some cases I have known a compost to be sopping wet at the top while remaining bone dry at the bottom. Allow the pots to drain, then return them to their pot holders. In most cases it is a mistake to stand plants in a water filled pot holder after a time the roots may be damaged. Pot holders are just an insurance against water running out of the drainage hole and damaging the carpet or furniture. In warm, bright weather a plant will need more water than during a dull cold period – water them according to weather, season and state of growth.

Composts

In due course, plants will need re-potting, so choosing the right compost for each operation is important – a mature plant needs a richer mixture than a tiny seedling.

Though there must be many house plants which are growing in a compost made up with ordinary garden soil, it is best to use a mixture specially devised to suit the particular needs of a wide range of plants. Unsterilised garden soil could quite easily contain pests or diseases, and under continuous watering quickly loses structure.

Proprietory composts can be divided into two groups; those with loam as the basic ingredient, and the other, these days the larger proportion, which are peat based. Loam, which is the gardener's way of describing the top 4 inches of turf from old pasture land, which has been stacked for 18 months to rot down, is becoming increasingly hard to procure. Peat makes an acceptable alternative.

For those fortunate people who can get good loam a general purpose compost devised by the John Innes Research Station has the following ingredients:
    7 parts sterilised loam,
    3 parts granulated medium grade peat,
    2 parts coarse sand.
The loam is sterilised either by treating it with heat or chemicals to kill weeds, pests, and diseases. Fertilizer can then be added to suit the needs of each individual plant.

For young seedlings or cuttings, to each 15 lbs of compost add 1 ounce (28 grams) John Innes Base Fertilizer plus ³/₁₆ ounce (5 grams) of chalk. The chalk is left out if potting Azalea, Camellia, or similar lime hating plants. This is known as the JOHN INNES NO 1 COMPOST.

For older plants the basic mixture remains the same but the amount of fertilizer and chalk added is doubled. This is known as the JOHN INNES NO 2 COMPOST.

For fully mature plants growing in large pots the amount of fertilizer and chalk added is trebled. This in turn is known as the JOHN INNES NO 3 COMPOST.

Unless large quantities of compost are needed it is much easier to go out and buy a bag with all the ingredients already mixed together.

Peat based composts are suitable for most house plants, but as with those based on loam it is safer to buy them ready mixed. Usually the basic ingredients are peat and coarse sand; to these are added all the nutrients which a plant needs to keep it in balanced growth. Loamless composts are cleaner to handle and drain better than those containing loam but once they get really dry it is difficult to get them moist again. With peat based mixtures use a plastic pot and start feeding 6–8 weeks after potting. The reason for the early feeding is that the fertilizer in peat based compost is soon leached by regular watering, and, unlike loam, neither peat nor sand contain many supplementary nutrients. My own general rule when potting off a plant is to use a loam based compost for vigorous plants which develop strong roots, and peat based mixtures for the remainder.

1

2

3

Hydroponics

The compost is really just a way of supporting the plant and a readily available cheap carrier for the fertilizer. By growing the plants in a container filled with water to which has been added all the chemicals a plant requires, the need for soil, feeding, potting and watering is done away with. For my first attempt at soil-less cultivation I used an old fashioned goldfish bowl and some cuttings of the green and white striped Tradescantia. After spacing the cuttings out across the container I used aquarium gravel to hold them in place, just about to half way up the sides. I then filled the bowl with water in which a packet of proprietory fertilizer had been dissolved (1). At regular intervals I stripped the system down thoroughly, rinsed the gravel, scrubbed out the bowl, replaced plants and gravel plus a fresh supply of nutrient solution. I developed a more luxurious system putting the roots of the plant inside a perforated funnel which had once done duty inside a tea urn. I chose a Chlorophytum for the experiment simply because they are easy to grow and there was a good stock to choose from. After filling the cylinder with pea gravel to anchor the 'Spider Plants' (Chlorophytum) roots I plunged it into a bowl half filled with the water/fertilizer mixture (2). Having the plant in a separate pot made routine maintenance much easier. All I did was lift it out, rinse, clean and refill the bowl before starting the process all over again.

Modern techniques have advanced way beyond my primitive home-made hydroculture bowl. Water level indicators, filler tubes, special granules manufactured for use in hydroponics to just the right size for efficient capillary action (3). One mistake the newcomer to soil-less gardening makes is to assume that a plant can be transferred direct from loam or peat based compost to a water fertilizer solution. Far better to grow plants from seed or cuttings specifically for hydroculture in such a way that they develop the special root system which enables them to accept the nutrient solution with a minimum of discomfort. I do this by potting them up after washing the roots free of compost in coarse sand or the material made specifically for the purpose which looks like compressed boiler ash, in granules the size of a finger nail, or vermiculite. The inner pot is made of open mesh plastic, while the container which holds it is waterproof. Usually, after about 5 weeks the water roots are developed enough for them to be put into one of the specially manufactured hydroponic systems. Once made up the system will survive without attention for up to a fortnight, ideal for holidays.

Potting and Re-potting

There is an understandable reluctance on the part of someone
with a healthy pot plant to risk harming it by actually
knocking it out and re-potting it in another container. After a
while, however, roots do become so tightly packed inside the
narrow confines of a pot, that unless they are given a larger
container and fresh compost to feed on they will die. Do not
wait until the plant is obviously unhappy before re-potting,
by that time it is usually too late. Fortunately, it is quite a
simple matter to remove the plant from a pot by putting one
hand over the surface of the soil (letting the plant stick
through between the fingers) turning it upside down and
giving a sharp tap on the base of the pot (1), or tap the rim
against a potting bench/table ledge. Examine the roots to see
if they are forming a web over the compost round the pot edge
(2). If they are, re-pot, if not, just drop the root ball back into
the same pot. A couple of sharp taps on the bench settles
everything back in place.

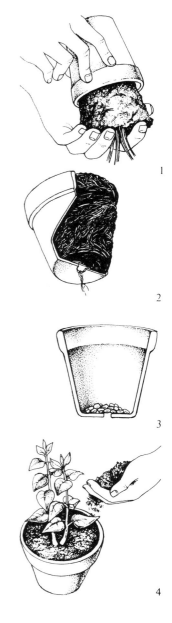

Quite often roots growing through the drainage hole are
sufficient proof that the plant is pot bound. Moving a plant
into a pot just an inch or so larger is usually sufficient. Over
potting is a mistake, it is wasting compost and if the roots do
not occupy the available space quickly enough, that too is
detrimental. A young plant in a 60 pot (9cm) could be moved
into a 48 (11cm) pot. A useful check is to place a pot of the
same size that the plant is already growing in inside one of the
new size, and the new compost added around the pot. The
smaller pot is then lifted out to reveal a hole in the compost
which is roughly the same size as the plant's root ball.

When a plant is growing in a loam based compost/clay pot,
pot on into the same kind of pot and mixture. The same
principle applies with the peat based/plastic container. Use
only absolutely clean pots. I try to wash mine before storing
them away as it saves a lot of time.

Put a handful of gravel or a piece of old pot over the drainage
hole if you are using clay pots (3). With plastic containers I
have never found 'crocking', as it is termed, makes much
difference to the drainage. Next, a thick layer of compost,
then knock out the plant as described. Drop it into the
prepared pot, adjust the depth so that the top of the old
compost ball comes just below the finished level of the new
compost when potting is completed (4). Fill the gap between
the pot side and root ball and firm with the fingers or a pot
rammer – made from a flat sided piece of wood. Peat based
mixtures should only be pressed gently with the fingers.

11

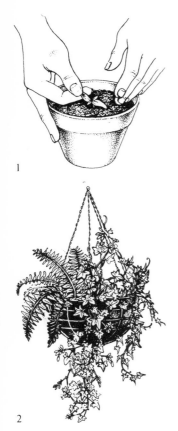

Containers

I only tease out the old root ball if the plant is very pot bound or if re-potting into a container the same size. In the case of pot bound plants it helps to encourage re-rooting if the old roots are untangled and those which are dead or damaged cut away. When re-potting into the same sized pot, I remove as much of the old compost that safety allows to make room for the new. After re-potting is completed, give the plant a thorough watering to settle it down, and keep it close for a few days in warmer, more humid conditions to recover.

Potting off as opposed to potting on is slightly different as it usually means moving cuttings or seedlings from a seed tray into individual pots. Hold seedlings by the leaf (1), never by the stem, and correctly position them in the pot before filling round with compost (1) and firming. With cuttings which have soft, new formed roots extra care must be taken when firming or the fragile roots might be damaged. A thorough watering will settle the compost round the roots better than anything else.

All my plants are grown in standard sized pots to make best use of space in the greenhouse, but these would certainly not look very ornamental dotted about a living room or bathroom. Indoors the plants are placed inside ornamental bowls or troughs so the rough plastic or clay finish is hidden. Anything will serve for a plant holder but do remember that too wide a diversity of shapes and colours in one room will reduce the overall effect to something closely approximating a jumble sale. A good plant can be made to look even more impressive by being placed in the right container. A wall bracket or macramé holder for plants which hang down, or a home-made hanging basket (2) will add colour in a south facing window when filled with suitable plants. In such a situation I try to use trailing plants so as to mask the hard edges of the basket.

There are various types of self-watering pots and troughs which might enable people who are away from home for several days at a time to grow house plants satisfactorily. These are containers of different shapes which fit over a small tray filled with water. A wick leads from the water reservoir to a capillary mat or similar plunge material to keep the plants above evenly moist (3). All the labour then required is to keep the water tray topped up.

One treat, which most house plants enjoy, is to be stood outside on a warm day when it is raining. A brisk shower freshens up the foliage better than the most sophisticated chemical cleaner.

Easy to grow plants (foliage)

There are some plants which are so resilient they will adapt to and grow under almost any conditions. No one, however, can give guarantees when dealing with living material, least of all with plants which continue to fascinate and confound me at the same time.

I know one enthusiast who grows 'African Violets' superbly on shelves over radiators, and yet considers it an achievement if a Cyclamen survives in her care for more than a fortnight. Another house I visited recently sported a Cyprepedium acaule in full bloom on a kitchen windowsill which I was assured had been potted for years in soil shovelled from the rose beds. Just as some gardens suit one shrub more than another, so do some houses prove more agreeable to a particular type of pot plant. Part of the excitement of growing plants indoors lies in experimenting.

There are so many plants available, and a walk around any well stocked nursery hardly seems to help when everything looks in robust health. So the following are six foliage and six flowering house plants which would make a solid base on which to start a collection. All are popular and generally available.

Chlorophytum comosum 'Variegatum' 'Spider Plant'

I wonder how many thousands of gardeners were first introduced to the absorbing hobby of house plant cultivation by a present of a 'Spider Plant' as it is popularly known. Certainly if there is a prize for plants so tough and indestructible then this must be one of the top contenders. One specimen I looked after for twenty years spread off-spring from Norfolk to an isolated farm on the Cheviots, so freely did it produce plantlets. The long arching straplike leaves are striped green and white which develop best when shaded from direct sunshine. During late spring, early summer, long wiry stems grow in very much the same way as strawberries, and at the end of each one a small plantlet develops (1). These, as would be expected, are easy enough to root just pegged down with a paper clip into a pot of compost (2). Once rooted the runner is detached from the parent. When in full growth from early March to mid September water frequently and every ten days give a liquid feed. With most house plants a weak liquid fertilizer applied every ten to fourteen days is of greater benefit than a strong feed at less frequent intervals.

Re-potting and division (3) of over large plants is best carried out in spring just as growth begins. The temperature in winter is not critical providing it never drops below 40–45 degrees F.

Ficus elastica 'Decora' 'Rubber Plant'

This is one of the very popular house plants, requiring only a modest amount of attention to keep it healthy. Probably better known as 'Rubber Plant', the large glossy green leaves develop that healthiest sheen away from direct sunlight, so they can stand back from the window. Avoid high temperatures, which, if accompanied by a dry atmosphere will discolour the leaves. A minimum winter temperature of 55–60 degrees F is adequate. I am convinced that it is incorrect watering that does the most harm. Keep the soil just moist in winter which is the resting period; water often in the growing season – April to September, and feed once a week. Sponge the leaves with lukewarm water to keep them free of dust. This improves their appearance and keeps them functioning properly. Re-potting may be done during April, using any standard compost.

The simplest method of propagation, particularly with an old plant which is growing too tall, is to make an air layer. Make a cut 1½–2 inches long, 10 inches or so from the top of the plant. Put a match stalk in before withdrawing the knife to keep the wound open (1), then paint the cut with rooting powder. Take some moist sphagnum moss; wrap this round the wounded stem (2) and bind it in place with polythene to make it air tight (3). Within a few weeks roots will sprout from the cuts, and when these are large enough the layer can be cut off and potted up in a peat based compost. Do not firm or the roots which are very soft will be broken. Propagation is difficult by leaf/bud or stem cuttings unless they are kept in a heated propagating case. A deep box over a radiator in a window recess makes a good bottom heated propagation unit.

When a complete growing tip is removed for rooting you do get a well shaped plant but on a one for one basis. By taking a small section of the stem with a leaf and bud (4) attached it is possible to get from one rubber plant with twenty leaves an equal number of rooted cuttings and as a result is very popular with commercial growers. To save space in the propagating frame roll the leaves up and tie them with soft wool. Unless care is taken, leaf cuttings will grow at an angle, but by potting so that the elbow is below compost level the malformation is hidden. Even a polythene bag will function as a propagation frame. Bed the leaf or tip cuttings in a pot filled with the peat sand compost, enclose the whole in a polythene bag and suspend it over a radiator so it gets heat without being scorched. Encourage rooting by dipping any cuttings in rooting powder before inserting them in the compost.

Hedera (various) 'Ivy'

There are advantages in growing one or two house plants which are almost hardy and capable of growing in poor light. This, no doubt, explains why the forms of common Ivy are so popular. They adapt so readily to a sudden drop in temperature. Poor light may cause variegated leaved varieties to produce plain green foliage, but the balance is quickly restored by placing it on a windowsill.

They can be trained up a trellis (1) or the shoots look equally attractive hanging over the pot rim (2). Keep the compost well watered from late March to September, liquid feed every three weeks during the same period. In winter allow the compost to get fairly dry between waterings, but not arid, and do not feed at all. Re-pot into fresh compost every second year, just as growth begins in March. There are several varieties to choose from: 'Chicago Variegata' with cream and green leaves, 'Goldchild' with leaves so heavily variegated they are more gold than green, and 'Heisse' with glaucous green leaves edged with silver are splendid value. Rooted cuttings which are easily propagated can be used either indoors or planted out in the garden.

Of all the 'Ivies' grown as house plants a form of the Canary Island Ivy 'Gloire de Marengo' is my favourite with foliage coloured a mixture of dark green, through silver to creamy white. Though not hardy outdoors it makes a most attractive room decoration. This rather choice Ivy requires the same treatment as the common Ivy but must be kept frost free. Cuttings taken during the summer are easy enough to root. To keep a specimen bushy and well furnished with leaves pinch out the growing tips of any side shoots which appear (3). Sponging the leaves regularly with luke warm water keeps them free from dust.

Philodendron scandens (oxycardium) 'Sweetheart Plant' or 'Parlour Ivy'

A resilient house plant with bright green, heart shaped leaves which grow on slender stems.

During summer keep the pot well watered and give a fertilizer feed every 14–21 days. From September to February reduce the water supply so that the compost is only just moist and do not feed. Pinch out young shoots which grow too vigorously – they need not be wasted but can be rooted as cuttings. To propagate, make sections of a stem with a leaf and bud attached. Bury the stem horizontally in the compost with the leaf showing above. Within a short space of time, usually a few weeks, roots should form.

Pilea cadierei 'Nana' 'Aluminium Plant'

One of the most tolerant, easy plants for a beginner to start a collection with. The dark green puckered leaves are highlighted with silver patches in a most becoming way. Apply water freely during the growing season – March to August, but reduce the supply during the winter so that the soil is kept just moist. Maintain a winter temperature above 50 degrees F which in my experience is a great deal less than most gardeners will put up with themselves.

Cuttings of young shoots taken in early summer root very easily, so propagation is no problem. Re-potting is necessary once a year and is best carried out in April. Start feeding about 6 weeks after re-potting and continue at fortnightly intervals until September. Stand the plant in good light but not direct sunlight. A north-facing windowsill is ideal. When the stems get too tall and 'leggy', just cut them hard back to a suitable leaf joint (1).

Zebrina pendula 'Wandering Jew' or 'Zebra Plant'

The 'Wandering Jew' or 'Zebra Plant' has the easy going Latin American temperament which its homeland Mexico would suggest. A virtually indestructible cosmopolitan plant as much at home growing on a kitchen windowsill as on a patio shelf, it can cope with low winter temperatures and considerable neglect. A place in good light, but not direct sunlight brings out the full beauty of the leaves which are pale green with a silver stripe down the centre. Underneath they are green flushed purple.

Keep this plant well watered in summer but only just moist in winter. Re-pot into a proprietory compost each spring, and give a liquid feed every 14 days commencing six weeks after re-potting. Pinch back any long trailing shoots (2) – the tips can be used as cuttings, and will root in two weeks just standing in a glass of water (3). Plant these rooted cuttings three to a pot and you will have a large plant much quicker than when they are potted up singly. Overwatering in winter will make the foliage lose colour as will growing the plant in a dark corner.

The form of Zebrina pendula called 'Quadricolour' has white striped purple leaves which are deep purple underneath and look well in any suspended arrangement.

Another good form is Zebrina purpusii and this can give lavender flowers in late summer early autumn.

Zebrina is an ideal plant to grow in a hanging basket because here it has ample room for both root and leaf growth.

Easy to grow plants (flowering)

Campanula isophylla 'Italian Bell Flower'

The 'Italian Bell Flower' is particularly useful as the trailing, flowering stems make it an ideal basket or wall bracket plant. The best I have ever seen as a display were grown in a plant candelabra hanging in a picture window. The cool brightly lit position made the plants produce billowing masses of bell shaped flowers, and as both blue and white forms were included the effect was striking.

'Bell Flowers' need ample water and a liquid feed every ten days when in flower. In winter water only when the compost get really dry, and keep the pot standing in an unheated, frost free room – a minimum temperature of 40 degrees F is sufficient. Each year re-pot into a soil based compost. Tease away as much of the old soil as possible (1), because like most plants which come from the mountain areas it appreciates a free draining compost.

1

Propagate new stock by division of the root when re-potting (2), or by means of cuttings made from young shoots (3) in the spring. The combination of blue or white flowers and grey green foliage is deliciously cool on a hot July day.

I always take extra cuttings on the principle that a plant of such quality always comes in useful. I do not know of a better edging to a window box than Campanula isophylla. Plant two blue to one white and the long trailing growths hang over to hide the straight edge of the container. They are happy in the light, airy conditions which a patio or garden room provides, and will continue flowering throughout the summer. There is a variety called 'Mayii' which produces mauve flowers, but the white or blue are more equable in temperament.

2

Chrysanthemum

Until recently the flower colour and pungent fragrance of the Chrysanthemum were the very essence of autumn. By controlling the amount of light, and treating the cuttings with a special chemical which inhibits the growth of stem, nurserymen can offer Chrysanthemums for sale all the year round. When buying, the best plants to choose are those where the majority of flower buds are just showing colour with the outer petals unfurled but the centres still in tight bud.

There are two reasons why the buds turn brown and fail to open: insufficient light and too wet compost. Keep them adequately watered but do not allow them to stand in water. Any surplus which runs into the pot holder must be poured away. Do not feed – it should not be necessary and can upset growth. Given good conditions – light, cool and airy they will flower over several weeks.

3

1

2

3

Cyclamen persicum

The ever popular Cyclamen is one of the loveliest presents either to give or receive, combining as it does attractively marbled leaves and brightly coloured, elegant flowers. A cool even temperature is essential, and a position in good light but not direct sunlight. A minimum winter temperature of 55 degrees F is adequate.

Allow the compost to become quite dry between waterings but not so arid that the foliage wilts. I water cyclamen by standing the pot in an inch of water and allow this to rise by capillary action (1). This makes certain the root ball is evenly and thoroughly moist without any risk of the flower buds or the corm becoming too wet. As the flower buds start to show give a liquid feed every 10–14 days. Dead leaves or flowers should be removed so no stump is left to rot. As the flowers fade, gradually reduce the watering and keep the compost dry during the summer. In July water the compost, then as growth starts re-pot using any of the standard composts.

The easiest way to build up a good stock of flowering plants is by raising them from seed. One leading seed firm will make this even easier by offering the seed already sprouted (2). My last consignment arrived carefully packed between moist felt with the first leaf just showing. I potted them into peat based compost and all of them are growing strongly.

Hippeastrum

If flowers are wanted to open around Christmas time it is best to buy prepared bulbs. These are bulbs which have been grown in a particular way to encourage early flowering. Plant them in October and grow in a room temperature of 65 degrees F. In subsequent years the bulbs should be re-potted every other autumn, using any of the proprietory potting composts. Position the bulbs so that two thirds is buried below the surface (3). Stand the pot in good light and just damp the compost until growth begins, gradually increase the water as the flower buds grow, an indication that the roots are also active. A liquid feed can be given every ten days until the flowers open. As the leaves turn yellow stop watering and feeding. Should the foliage remain green as it sometimes does, keep the compost just moist – the flowers will open slightly earlier than those from the dried off bulbs.

The pot can stand outside during the summer. I put my Hippeastrum in a sheltered corner in early June and bring them back into shelter sometime in mid-September.

Propagation is by means of offsets pulled from around the parent bulb when re-potting.

Euphorbia pulcherrima 'Poinsettia'

Few pot plants can rival the brilliance of Poinsettia when the scarlet leaf-like bracts surrounding the insignificant flowers are fully developed. Over recent years the range of colour has been extended to include varieties with pink, white and creamy yellow bracts. Like the Chrysanthemum the Poinsettia can be treated with a chemical to stunt the stem length to make the plant compact. The normal flowering season is during the winter, but by keeping the plants in a dark room for 12–14 hours each day for 8 or 9 weeks flowers and bracts will appear out of season.

1

Avoid too high temperatures which cause the bracts to fade quickly. A winter minimum of 55 degrees F will suffice rising to 65 degrees F during the day. Keep the compost well watered with luke warm water until flowering is completed. As the leaves turn yellow water less frequently until almost dried off. In May prune back the top shoots (1) and re-pot into one of the proprietory composts. A constant temperature, good light and correct watering will help the bracts retain their colour for several months.

The plants are never as beautifully coloured in my experience when cut back and grown on for a second year. Instead of letting the young shoots which develop when the plant is pruned grow on, they can be taken and rooted as cuttings. Wait until they are about 5 inches long before removing them with a sharp knife (2). Allow the milky substance which oozes from the cut to dry before dipping the base of the shoot in rooting powder. The best rooting compost I have discovered is the mixture of 2 parts sharp lime free sand, 1 part peat. Dibble the cuttings in to a clay pot filled with compost and keep them in a warm moist place. An alternative would be to put the pot in a polythene bag (3) and the cuttings root in as little time as 5 weeks. Once rooted they may be potted off and grown on in John Innes potting compost.

2

Primula acaulis

Since childhood primroses have been for me the prelude to spring. A cool airy room with full light is the most suitable place to keep them. They will tolerate high temperatures, but this forces flowering and the leaves turn yellow sooner. To keep the air around them humid stand the pots on a tray of moist pebbles or plunge them in moist peat. A liquid feed every 14 days is usually sufficient to maintain balanced healthy growth. When flowering is finished, Primroses can be gradually hardened off, and then when the weather is suitable, planted outdoors, for once established they are hardy.

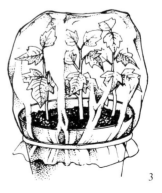

3

Feature Plants

A fine piece of furniture or an ornament can lend character to a room. In much the same way a well chosen plant becomes a focal point. Because there are so many plants to choose from, the novice, confused by a meaningless jumble of names flounders and frequently buys something which is totally unsuitable. A house offers almost the same opportunity for plant association and design as the garden outdoors. In the open garden a tree to be viewed across a broad sweep of lawn is chosen because it displays an individual character which compliments the garden design. A plant used as a focal point in a room should be selected on the same terms. Those most frequently used are usually evergreen with attractive foliage. Flowering plants are generally for short term effect, moved into the room when in full bloom not to compete with the permanent features, but for a brief while to compliment them. As a general guide remember green leafed plants enjoy shady positions but variegated forms enjoy good light but not long periods of sunshine.

Massed groups of flowering plants are exciting, stimulating interludes only, the calm undertone is supplied by the beautiful leaves and overall shape of the resident feature plants. When choosing a plant, the overriding factor should be what sort of conditions will the room or situation provide. Is the temperature cool, temperate or hot, is there plenty of light or does the plant need to be shade tolerant. There are many factors to be considered, but for just about every permutation of site there is a plant which will grow there. I became convinced of this after watching a 'Swiss Cheese Plant', Monstera, not only survive but grow in a studio where, admittedly the temperature was constant, but daylight was virtually non existent. The two people who owned the plant had endowed it with human characteristics even to the extent of talking to it. I found it strange that this was the only plant in the building, and as in so many houses care and attention is lavished on two or three plants when it would take very little more effort to grow a dozen.

A good feature plant should grow well in the conditions provided without needing special attention. Equally important it must be pleasing to the eye and compliment the other room decorations. Most people confessed when interviewed that they buy plants for the house on impulse, rarely setting out to buy a pre-chosen plant because it suits the room. This probably explains why indoor gardening is usually confined to the living room and kitchen. There are enough plants which will suit every room and situation. All the home gardener has to do is pick the right one for the right location.

Aralia sieboldii – Fatsia japonica

This quick growing plant has imposing 5–7 lobed leaves (1) which will even stand slight frost. A fairly cool position in half shade will enable the leaves to develop that dark green glossy sheen which gives the Aralia such a commanding presence. Copious amounts of water from late April to late August, plus a fortnightly feed will encourage rapid growth. Pot grown specimens 3 feet high are not uncommon. Cuttings of sucker-like growths from around the base of the plant (2) are easy to root. Re-pot in early March into a standard compost.

This is an invaluable plant for the flower arranger and when it gets too large for the house you can plant it outside in a sheltered position. A well grown specimen will soften the angular lines of a stair landing, or provide a welcome break in a long straight corridor.

Araucaria heterophylla (A. excelsa) 'Norfolk Island Pine'

The 'Norfolk Island Pine' (3) is really popular indoors. The soft rather fern like foliage and shape reminiscent of a Christmas tree are attractive in the shady corner of a garden-room, or entrance hall. Grown in company with Fuchsia which like similar cool airy conditions the 'Norfolk Island Pine' contributes to a harmonious design.

Keep well watered in summer but apply only enough to keep the soil moist in winter. Liquid feed once a month and re-pot in a proprietory compost every other spring during February. Though 'Norfolk Island Pine' can be pruned hard back it never makes a good shape afterwards. The young shoots can be rooted by using a heated propagating frame, grown on and the old plant discarded.

Asparagus plumosus (setaceus) 'Asparagus Fern'

The enormous specimen of Asparagus fern that graced a north facing window in my grandmother's house was the 'Jack's Beanstalk' of my childhood. That the room was unheated except on special occasions made the plants robust good health more remarkable. The elegant feathery branches (4) develop best under cool partially shaded conditions.

Water to capacity in summer but keep the compost on the dry side during winter. Re-pot each alternate March and apply a liquid fertilizer every three weeks from April to August.

Light foliage plants are useful in a north window or to lighten a sombre background, dark curtains or panelling.

This plant is an ideal beginner's plant as it will grow in a variety of conditions of warmth, light and humidity.

1

2

3

4

21

1

2

3

4

Asplenium nidus 'Birds Nest Fern'

The 'Birds Nest Fern' (1) has dark green leaves which look as if they have been varnished; the leaf stalk in contrast is often dark brown. A shady position is most suitable with plenty of water during the summer, but keep the compost nearly dry in the winter. Feed with liquid fertilizer once a fortnight during May, June and July. A position which catches just the evening sunlight is desirable, the long rays illuminating the highly polished leaves. I have found that re-potting every other spring is sufficient.

Begonia coccinea 'Angelwing'

'Angelwing' (2) has a special significance for me. A specimen was presented to me just as we started renovating the house and shared in all the upheaval, seeming to thrive on a diet of plaster, dust and cool temperature. In a room which has two windows, south and north, the Begonia spends summer on the north side and winter on the south. The leaves borne on long dark red stems are dull green, margined with red. Drooping clusters of pink flowers open from May, right through to December. Water heavily in summer and sponge the leaves to keep them dust free. In winter keep just moist with a minimum temperature of 50 degrees F. Three liquid feeds during summer are enough if the plant is re-potted in standard compost each year. In spring cut back any stems which have grown too long. Take cuttings in the summer.

Begonia metallica

Begonia metallica (3) is equally impressive and will grow in similar conditions with the same treatment. The green leaves are overlaid with silver and the crimson veins show to advantage when viewed against the light.

Although a humid atmosphere is essential or the leaves go brown, it will stand quite low temperatures – down to 45 degrees F provided the compost is kept only just moist.

Cissus antarctica 'Kangaroo Vine'

The 'Kangaroo Vine' (4) planted outdoors in my garden has survived two winters. An easily pleased climber with dark green leaves which are bronze tinted when young. By restricting the root in a small container growth can be stunted, otherwise, given a rich compost it behaves rather like its popular name and leaps quickly up to 8 or 10 feet in height.

Water regularly in summer but keep just moist in winter. Cuttings of shoot tips root easily in a sand compost. The long shoots are seen to advantage when trained over an alcove.

Dieffenbachia picta 'Exotica' 'Dumb Cane'

An attractive foliage plant which makes demands on the patience and purse of the indoor gardener to keep it in good order. Warmth, partial shade and careful watering are the three prime requisites, so a bathroom is usually a choice location for this plant. Clusters of oblong, creamy white and green variegated leaves grow from robust succulent stems.

Give them plenty of water during the growing season – March to August – only enough to keep the leaves turgid in winter. Re-pot every year in a good proprietory compost. Propagate by stem cuttings; cut a piece of stem into 1½ inch sections (1), or alternatively a growing tip (2). Both methods are only practical when the plant has lost its lower leaves and is then only fit for breaking up into cuttings.

The sap of 'Dumb Cane' is reputedly poisonous, so as a precaution wash after handling leaves etc.

Fatshedera lizei

The 'Fat Headed Lizzie' (3) is a roly poly good natured plant. The palmate leaves are a lustrous, shiny green, 6 inches across with 7 or 9 lobes. As would be expected from a hydrid created by crossing a shrub with a climber, the long stems do need support if grown to their full height of 6–8 feet but by pruning the tips out of the top shoots a dwarfer habit is formed. Minimum temperature 33 degrees F – just above freezing.

A liquid feed once a month from March to August, water sparingly and never enough to saturate the compost. In winter be even more miserly with moisture application. Cuttings of young shoots root readily in summer.

This is a handsome plant for a stairway, corner of the hall, or to relieve a bare wall in a large room.

Ficus benjamina

The 'Weeping Fig' (4) is a complete contrast to the more popular 'Rubber Plant' which is the most easily recognisable member of the Ficus family. The side branches covered in slender, pointed leaves arch out and down in graceful curves. Pale green at first, the leaves darken with age but always look fresh polished. Few plants are more tolerant of hard pruning. A humid atmosphere, a minimum temperature of 45 degrees F, and plenty of moisture during the period March to September will be found appropriate. Liquid feed 3 times in the growing season and re-pot every two years. Cuttings taken of young wood in June-July root easily. This is an ideal plant for a hall or foyer.

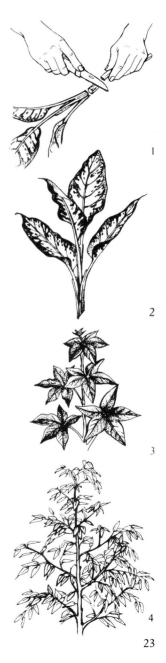

1

2

3

4

1

Ficus elastica 'Rubber Plant'

For a detailed description see page 14.
The variegated forms of 'Rubber Plant' (1) are deservedly popular but not quite so easy to grow as the plain foliaged. Try the marbled foliaged Ficus elastica 'Schryveriana' as being one of the easiest to please.

Hedera 'Gloire de Marengo'

The only Ivy which I have made a feature of with decoratively marbled green on cream leaves. Most effective in open plan living rooms, where by careful training and pruning it can be persuaded to provide a barrier between two areas.

Water regularly from March to September with liquid feed every three weeks. In winter keep the compost fairly dry. Re-pot in March every other year. Cuttings of the long shoots laid into moist compost will root.

2

Howea forsteriana 'Kentia' or 'Paradise Palm'

The tall stems are crowned with leaves which are divided into several leaflets which arch out like a peacock tail (2). Kentia are useful because they are amongst the most shade tolerant plants. The elegant leaves show to advantage when rising out of a dense packed mass of ferns and Pilea which are also shade tolerant. A minimum winter temperature of 55 degrees F with the soil just moist is adequate. In summer water freely from April to early August and give regular fortnightly feeds. Re-pot as required, about every 2 years in loam based compost with an extra part of peat to every 2 parts of standard mixture.

3

Hoya carnosa 'Wax Plant'

The 'Wax Plant' is a fairly vigorous climber with tough leathery, dark green leaves but in the form 'Variegata' they are delicately margined with yellow. During summer pinky white flowers (3) appear but it is the wax-like texture of the petals that earn the plant its popular name.

A light, well ventilated room, but not in bright sunlight is suitable with a minimum winter temperature of 50 degrees F. The Hoya needs generous quantities of water from April to August with a fortnightly liquid feed but keep the compost just moist in winter. There are no fixed rules in regard to re-potting, but I do so each April using John Innes No 1 compost. Cuttings of ripe wood will root but take rather a long time and I prefer to use a peat based compost for this purpose.

Monstera deliciosa 'Swiss Cheese Plant'

The 'Swiss Cheese Plant' is readily identifiable by the large, leathery, dark green leaves which are cut into segments almost to the mid-rib (1). The plant's habit of growing ariel roots along the stem can be used to advantage by training them along a cane or support wrapped in sphagnum moss. They need lots of water in summer, also sponge the leaves daily in hot weather. Feed at three week intervals and re-pot every second year. Keep the compost just moist during winter and maintain a temperature of 55 degrees F. Cuttings of the growing tips or stem sections with a leaf attached are two methods of propagation.

Remember Monstera do dislike cold draughts and excess water. A good check for overwatering in winter is to examine the leaves. If these are beaded with moisture the compost is too wet.

1

Neanthe bella or Chamaedorea elegans 'Parlour Palm'

Some nurseries list under one name, others under another but of the two Chamaedorea elegans is the most popular. The long leaf stalks which grow out from a tubular stem are furnished with narrow, leathery leaves for most of their length (2). Good light in a cool airy situation suits the 'Parlour Palm' with a winter minimum temperature of not less than 55 degrees F. Adequate water and a daily sponge or spray may be given in summer but keep the compost just damp in winter. Re-pot each year until the plant reaches maturity, then just top up each April, by carefully removing the top layer of compost and replacing it with John Innes No 2 mixture. Liquid feed every three weeks from April to August.

2

Philodendron bipinnatifidum

In addition to the 'Parlour Ivy' (P. scandens) described on page 15, P. bipinnatifidum or 'Green Fingered Plant' is another species with good foliage (3). It grows up to 3 feet high and the mature leaves are scalloped halfway to the mid-rib and wavy edged. In my experience this Philodendron is even more shade tolerant than the 'Parlour Palm' provided it is kept in a warm, humid atmosphere – 55 degrees F is essential. Unless the plant is in a naturally moist air, for example the bathroom, stand the pot on a tray of moist pebbles or plunge it in peat. Water heavily from April to August and spray the foliage over in really hot weather. Keep the compost just moist in winter. Propagation is not easy as the leaves grow on long stalks from a central rootstock, but division of the rootstock of older plants proves satisfactory.

3

1

2

3

Rhoicissus rhomboidea 'Grape Ivy'

A most attractive climbing plant which will grow well under cool shady conditions. I had a plant cut down by frost when the heating system failed, which responded to the untimely pruning by growing even more vigorously the following year. The diamond shaped leaves are toothed at the edges (1), hairy when young but turning glossy green with age. Keep the compost moist but never saturated and the atmosphere buoyant in a minimum temperature of 40–45 degrees F. Sponge the leaves and apply a liquid feed every three weeks. Re-pot using a John Innes No 2 compost in spring. Propagate by taking off young shoots in late spring – this is no real hardship to the plant as nipping back side shoots keeps the shape neat and upright.

The most effective use I have seen 'Grape Ivy' put to was when a well grown specimen was trained round a blocked up fireplace set in a primrose yellow painted wall.

Schefflera actinophylla 'Umbrella Tree'

The long leaflets which radiate from a central stem arch downwards like the ribs of an opened umbrella (2) as if the plant was perpetually short of water. Growth is fairly slow and it needs a situation in good light with the temperature above 55 degrees F. Direct sunlight discolours the foliage.

Keep the soil moist at all times and stand the pot on a tray of moist pebbles. A liquid feed at monthly intervals is usually sufficient, and re-pot alternate years in a loam based compost. Propagate only by seed which, even when obtainable, germinates erratically – at least when I have tried it!

Scindapsus aureus 'Devils Ivy'

The up to six inch long leaves are bright, vivid green, irregularly streaked with yellow. As the leaves get older they broaden to become almost heart shaped (3). As the climbing stems need support they can be used to good effect by training them across a trellis fitted to a wall bracket. A position in good light, but not in full sun with a temperature never less than 60 degrees F provides ideal conditions for the leaves to develop full colour. In cooler temperatures the plant soon sickens, particularly the varieties with heavily variegated leaves. In winter water very little, just enough to keep the soil moist, and even in summer the soil should never be too wet. Liquid feed once a month. Re-potting may be necessary each spring, but as the plant gets older every other year should be enough. Propagate by means of side shoots which should be taken off anyway when over long to keep the plant neat.

Cacti, Succulents and Bromeliads

In general these very specially adapted plants originate from the drier, less fertile regions. The exceptions included here are also different from the general run of indoor plants in that they are epiphytic which means in the wild they grow on a tree trunk or rock face. They all have one thing in common in adapting very well to house conditions. The shape is unusual, the flowers when they appear are often brilliantly coloured if short lived. Those mentioned require only a low winter temperature and are not seriously disturbed by a dry atmosphere. Cacti and Succulents need every glimmer of sunlight our climate affords so are best accommodated on a south facing window ledge or patio so long as it is heated enough to keep the frost out. They need little water in winter, sufficient only to keep them from shrivelling up. In bright hot summer weather a twice weekly application of water will not be excessive. Propagation, feeding or any special idiosyncrasies are mentioned under specific plants.

A lot of Cacti have spines which can cause painful or even poisonous wounds if carelessly handled, so wear gloves (1).

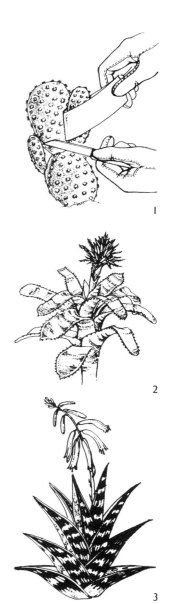

1

2

3

Aechmea fasciata 'Urn Plant'

The long, strap-like leaves which arch out from a central base (2) are glaucous green striped with silver grey. The flower spike which grows from the central tube has pink bracts which last a long time. In summer keep the compost evenly moist and the central funnel filled with water. In winter keep the compost just damp and the central funnel dry. A winter minimum temperature of 50 degrees F is warm enough. Propagate by removing the offshoots which grow out from the base of the plant and pot these up in a peat based compost. As the parent plant dies after flowering it is not essential to remove the young rosettes unless more plants are needed.

Aloe variegata 'Partridge Breast'

Aloe is a succulent, whose dark green triangular leaves (3) are marked at regular intervals with white bands. The leaf colour rather than the pale orange flower is the main attraction.

A place in the sun with a minimum temperature of 40 degrees F will keep the Aloe content. Water carefully at all times, even in winter when the plant is in growth the compost should be only just moist. Above all make sure no water gathers in the tufted leaves. Re-pot every other year in summer into a loam based compost with extra sharp sand added to give good drainage. Offsets, young shoots which grow at the base, can be removed at the same time for propagation.

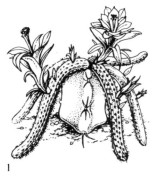

Aporocactus flagelliformis 'Rat's Tail'

The trailing grey green stemmed 'Rat's Tail' (1) is a very tough plant indeed. The pink flowers usually open in April and are best displayed when the pot is suspended in a hanging basket. A temperature which never falls below freezing, dry atmosphere and good light are all this undemanding plant requires. Water regularly in summer and enough to keep the compost just moist in winter. Re-pot each year in a proprietory compost with extra sand added. Cuttings of young shoots root well in sand or vermiculite.

Chamaecereus silvestrii 'Peanut Cactus'

The 'Peanut Cactus' is a neat, undemanding Argentinian which in April bears vermilion red funnel shaped flowers which seem astonishingly large for so small a plant (2). A west facing window is the best location. Keep the plant cool in winter – minimum 35 degrees F – with only enough moisture to prevent shrivelling. In fact, a cold dry winter is said to improve flowering. In summer water regularly allowing the compost to dry out on top before applying any more. Re-pot every 2 years in a gritty compost, pulling off the gherkin like stems for cuttings.

Echeveria retusa

Of the many Echeveria available this is the easiest one to grow and it flowers each spring. The fleshy grey green leaves form rosettes (3) which offer a ready means of propagation, as they root easily when detached from the parent plant. A sunlit windowsill, regular watering in the summer but very little moisture in the winter, is all the attention they need. Re-pot the plants each year into a standard loam based compost.

Echinocactus grusonii 'Golden Barrel'

The 'Golden Barrel' is like a pale green tub covered with yellow spines (4). Young plants present an almost smooth outline, then as they grow older the clefts deepen – a condition emphasised by the arrangements of the spiky growths (ariols) along the crest like ridge. Grown in a pot they do not often exceed 12 inches by as much across.

To achieve the sheen of good health it needs a place in full sun with a minimum temperature of 40 degrees F. Keep the compost moist in summer but allow it to almost dry out in winter. A layer of the pea gravel on top of the compost is a safeguard against rotting. Re-pot every other year in a compost of three parts standard loam to 1 part sharp grit or sand. Propagate by means of seed sown in March.

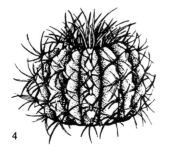

Echinocereus pectinatus

This develops large purplish pink flowers during late summer (1), granted it has a light airy situation. Water moderately in the summer but keep fairly dry in winter with a minimum temperature of 40 degrees F. Re-potting is necessary every second year using a mixture of 2 parts standard loam based compost to 1 part sharp sand or grit.

Epiphyllum x hybridum 'Orchid Cactus'

The 'Orchid Cactus' (2) is one of the most admired of the genus. It is easy to grow and exhibits large, silky textured, flowers during early summer. These range from red, yellow, pink and white. A place in good light but not direct sunlight – temperature 45 degrees F minimum. Water freely in summer but in winter keep compost just moist. A liquid feed as the buds show on the flattened leaf-like stems is worthwhile. They need re-potting every year as the flowers fade – either loam or peat based compost. Cuttings of the stems will root particularly if left to dry out for a day or two.

Euphorbia milii splendens 'Crown of Thorns'

The sparsely leaved, sharply thorned branches (3) are deep red but it is the bright scarlet bracts surrounding the yellow flowers which are the chief attraction. Full sunshine, really dry air and a buoyant climate are essential. So find a place in a south facing window with a winter temperature of not less than 55 degrees F. I stand the plant outside on a sheltered terrace for summer. Compost should be moist in summer and almost dry in winter. Cuttings made from the branch tips may be rooted in sharp sand.

Kalanchoe blossfeldiana 'Tom Thumb'

Full light and plenty of water in the summer suits Kalanchoe blossfeldiana whose dark green glossy leaves make a pleasant background to the orange red flowers which open in winter when the days are shortest (4) – minimum temperature 40 degrees F. Re-pot each spring in any standard compost and propagate by stem cuttings in June or by seed sown into a suitable compost during April.

The red flowers of this neat little pot plant are normally produced in late winter, early spring. By limiting the amount of daylight each plant gets, the flowers can be made to develop at almost any time of the year, especially for sale at Christmas time. Kalanchoe are easy to care for. They need regular watering in summer, but keep the compost only moist enough to prevent wilting in winter.

1

2

3

4

1

Lithops lesliei 'Pebble Cactus'

'Pebble Cactus' is well named. They really do resemble evenly formed stones. The leaves grow in pairs like partially opened fleshy lips, and the flowers grow in the central groove (1) – either white or yellow. They need good bright sunlight and a minimum temperature of 40 degrees F. Keep compost dry in winter, moderately moist from April to August. The old leaves dry up but fresh ones grow immediately. Re-pot every second or third year using a mixture of 2 parts standard compost, 1 part sharp sand. Propagate by means of seed sown in the same mixture in April.

Mammillaria 'Powder Puff'

Full sun is an essential aid to flowering, not just in the summer but in the winter as well which means growing them all the year round on a south facing window sill. Every two or three days turn the pots round so each side of the plant gets a proper share of light, otherwise growth is uneven. In winter the temperature must be kept above 45 degrees F, for though the plants will survive cooler conditions the risk of rotting at soil level is much greater. The compost needs to be just moist enough from September to February to prevent the plants shrivelling, in summer water regularly. Re-potting is best carried out each year in April using a compost of 2 parts loam based compost to 1 part of sharp sand.

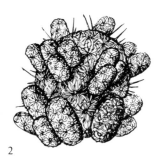

2

Mammillaria gracilis forms what can only be termed as a many branched clump (2). The mass of white spines give the plant a hoary appearance while the flowers are yellow tinged pink. The branches will root if pulled away then inserted in sharp sand.

Neoregelia carolinae 'Fingernail Plant'

Any house plant which shares in and survives the trauma of moving house becomes an honorary member of the family. At one stage my plant suffered near freezing temperatures in a partially demolished room, so for me Neoregelia carolinae is special and beautiful. Long shining green leaves grow from a central rosette which is tube-like (3). In due course, insignificant flowers grow from the tube, and the base of the surrounding leaves turn bright scarlet. Keep the central tube full of water in summer and the compost moist, but in winter hardly any water is needed, and the central tube is allowed to dry out. Propagate by means of the offsets which form around the base of the old rosette, these are detached and potted up in a peat based compost. The old rosette dies after flowering, at least this is my experience.

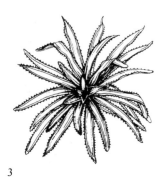

3

Opuntia microdasys 'Prickly Pear'

The flattened stem sections give it a curious doll-like appearance (1), but the covering of barbed bristles are sufficient deterrent to any over-affectionate, gestures. The glochids, as the barbs are called, can cause painful scratches so keep this plant well out of the reach of small children. Give it plenty of light, a high summer temperature and regular water, but in winter keep dry and maintain a temperature of not less than 40 degrees F. Re-pot every other year in April using a loam based compost plus extra sand. Cuttings of stem sections root better if they are left to dry out for a week.

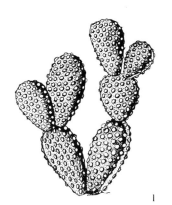

1

Rebutia kupperiana 'Red Crown Cactus'

During the summer trumpet shaped red flowers (2) grow out from the base of the plant. They like a well lit position in winter when the temperature should not fall below 40 degrees F. Keep the watering constant during summer but in winter reduce the supply until the compost is only just moist. Re-pot every second year in a loam based compost with extra sand. Propagate simply by detaching offsets during the summer or by sowing seeds.

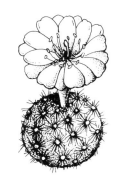

2

Rhipsalidopsis gaertneri 'Easter Cactus'

The 'Easter Cactus' is one of the better known species with tubular scarlet flowers which grow from the tip of the flattened stems. In my experience this cactus will tolerate a position in light shade, especially from hot summer sunshine when the pot can be stood outdoors in a sheltered, shaded corner. Keep it well watered in summer – May to November and liquid feed every 14 days. In winter water less often and do not feed. Minimum temperature 50 degrees F. Re-pot each year in the standard loam based mixture with extra peat added. Propagate by means of stem cuttings during the summer.

Sansevieria trifasciata 'Laurentii' 'Bowstring Hemp' or 'Mother-in-Law's Tongue'

This grows clusters of rigid, strap-like stalkless green leaves which are edged and banded with silver or cream stripes (3). Water moderately in summer, but during the winter keep the compost only slightly damp. My plants have survived 40 degrees F but 50 degrees F is a more agreeable minimum. Re-pot only when the stems become overcrowded usually every 3rd year, preferably in the spring. Propagate by division when re-potting. Leaves cut into sections will root but the yellow variegation is lost.

3

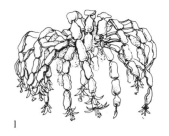

1

2

3

Schlumbergera truncata, Zygocactus, 'Christmas Cactus'

This plant is best grown either on a pedestal or hanging basket as the flat leaf-like branches hang down from the central trunk (1). The red trumpet shaped flowers which grow from the stem tips are then seen in full perspective. They prefer good light with shade from midsummer sun. A winter temperature of 50 degrees F is preferred but they will survive short periods of 40 degrees F in my experience. As the flower buds show, give plenty of water providing the temperature is kept at 55 degrees F or over, and liquid feed every 14 days. In summer I rest the plants for 6 to 8 weeks by reducing the water supply until the compost is just moist but not bone dry. Re-pot each year in spring or August using a standard potting compost with extra sand added. Propagate by means of stem cuttings.

Sedum sieboldii 'Variegatum'

'Cream Leaved Stonecrop' makes a useful edging plant for the indoor gardener. The flattened leaves are edged with red and have a yellow centre (2). Like all 'Stonecrops' they prefer good bright light with normal watering in summer, but in winter allow the compost to get almost dry. The mixture I use is 2 parts loam, 1 peat, 1 sand – the John Innes seed mixture suits very well. Propagation is by means of stem cuttings taken in May–June. In autumn stems die back to ground level – a habit which is most disturbing. Sometimes a plain green shoot appears amongst the variegated foliage, these should be removed or the whole plant may revert. In autumn reddish pink flowers develop. I use this as a guide to reducing the water supply for soon the stems die back.

Senecio rowleyanus 'String of Beads'

A macramé holder made from string or raffia which can be hung in a window forms an excellent method of showing off the trailing stems (3). It also permits the maximum pleasure from the fragrant flowers which open in early autumn. The creeping stems are furnished with small fleshy leaves, the white tufted flowers have a deep purple eye, but it is the fragrance which gives the most pleasure. Full sunlight and a winter minimum temperature above 50 degrees F will go a long way to ensuring success in growing this Senecio. Water normally from April to September and during the winter months keep the compost only just moist. Re-pot in spring into a loam based mixture with extra sand added. Stem cuttings which should be taken in mid summer are not difficult to root.

Vriesia splendens 'Flaming Sword'

The 'Flaming Sword Plant' makes a very useful dual purpose plant with rosettes of decorative foliage, then in due season a sword shaped spike of red and yellow bracts (1). A temperature which never falls below 55 degrees F is essential with good light but not full sun. Keep the leaf tube topped up with soft water during the summer and the compost moist without being saturated. After flowering allow the central tube to dry out for the winter. Sponge the leaves regularly or the beauty of the green and brown markings is hidden. Propagation is easily effected by means of offsets which form round the parent plant and potted up in a mixture of peat and sand.

1

Cacti and succulents are particularly suitable for planting up small indoor gardens. Unlike the more traditional house plant they do not demand regular watering or feeding to survive so will take no permanent harm if left unattended during the family holiday. All the occupants in the mini-garden should need similar growing conditions. The most attractive indoor garden I have seen was made up of a wooden plant trough just stained and varnished to bring out the grain of the wood, and fitted with a plastic liner. This is not so expensive as it may sound: the plastic liner was a standard green house pot holder and the wooden trough was made of planed white pine to fit it. Any ornamental container capable of holding compost will do, and for Cacti – 3–4 inches deep is enough.

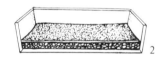

2

Put a thin layer of aquarium gravel in the bottom to act as drainage, drop in some lump charcoal to stop it from becoming stagnant. A thick layer of peat or a piece of the felt used on a capillary watering bench on the top of the gravel will stop the compost washing down into it (2). Then on top goes a thin layer of compost, a loam based John Innes mixture, plus to every 5 parts of compost 1 extra part of sharp sand and 1 of crushed brick. I prefer to start with a thin layer of compost, then I can put the plants out in their pots and move them around to get the best association. A few pieces of stone carefully included in the landscape will improve the effect. When the final position of all the plants is settled, knock each one out of its pot and bed in the compost until the finished level is about ½ inch below the container rim (3). Never have the compost flush with the rim, this leaves no room for watering or top dressing.

3

The most common pest among cacti and succulents is a mealy bug which leaves a whiteish deposit on the stem. Check by a malathion spray. The roots of the plant may be attacked by the root mealy bug and this can be controlled by regular re-potting and watering with a dilute solution of nicotine.

1

2

Lithops are best kept in a garden of their own, for they are well named 'Living Stones'. By raising a stock of plants from seeds the differences in shape and colour are sufficiently individual to be interesting. A collection I raised from seed sent by a friend in Mexico gave me enough plants to make up a garden which lasted several years.

Another idea is borrowed from a garden which has survived in a cottage whose only heating is a coal fire and a paraffin stove. The temperature must very often drop very close to freezing point in winter. The centre piece is a 'Partridge Breasted' Aloe which gives height at the back. A 'Rats Tail' cactus disguises one side of the stone containers, and a Kalanchoe or 'Tom Thumb' flowers at irregular intervals for most of the year (1).

Groups of 'Powder Puff' and 'Prickly Pear' seedlings offsets or cuttings set in a mini landscape of unusual shaped rocks make a most decorative feature on a light window sill (2). I like this combination because the flowers of the 'Powder Puffs' are handsome enough both individually and collectively.

There are many ways of starting children on a life long interest in gardening, one which I have found particularly effective is by arranging a cactus landscape. A bowl or dish will do so long as it has sufficient depth to hold the compost, the sides can be painted in attractive colours. Make up a compost as described in the Cacti section, then use pieces of coloured stone to contour the mini landscape. A small mirror let into the compost near the front of the container can portray a small lake. Choose plants which flower while fairly young – nothing kills a child's interest quicker than looking after a plant which never seems to do anything but grow. In this respect Rebutia are my own favourite. They flower abundantly when young, are easily raised from seed or pull-off cuttings and will survive a degree of ill treatment. In winter the compost must be kept dry and the temperature cool, even down to 40 degrees F is acceptable, then the plants will flower well. To make up the rest of the garden choose plants which enjoy the same conditions. Sedum sieboldii 'Variegatum' is not a cactus but can be included to hang over the edge of the pot. Opuntia to plant round the 'pool', because even though they rarely flower they have such a cactus look about them. Once established, given careful watering and top dressing a cactus garden will last for several years. Remember, cacti need more watering in summer than in winter. As a final embellishment I top dress round the plants with aquarium gravel.

Popular House Plants

I have grouped the plants under headings – Cool and Light, Cool with Shade, Warm with Shade, Warm and Light.

COOL AND LIGHT

Callistemon speciosus 'Bottle Brush'

The 'Bottle Brush' makes a showy pot plant growing eventually up to 6 feet high, but in a pot or tub it can be restricted to 3 feet and still carry a good crop of the scarlet flue brush flower spikes (1). Plenty of light and fresh air in summer, but cool and frost free in winter are this plant's main requirements. Moderate watering with soft water in summer, reduced even further in winter. Re-pot using a standard compost which is free of lime in spring.

Citrus mitis 'Dwarf Orange'

Properly trained this makes a neat bushy plant which has scented, white, thick petalled flowers. The miniature orange fruits are very ornamental (2), and to encourage the flowers to set, spray the bush with tepid water, preferably about midday. Keep the plants in good light always with a minimum temperature of 45 degrees F. A liquid feed at fortnightly intervals helps the fruit to swell. I also give the plants in full growth a salt spoonful of Epsom Salts (magnesium sulphate) twice a year. Re-pot every two or three years, but topdress with loam based acid compost every year. Cuttings taken with a heel of old wood in June–July are quite easy to root.

Pelargoniums

Pelargoniums grow best in cool places with good light. Both the 'Scented leaved Geranium', Pelargonium crispum 'Variegatum', and the 'Ivy Leaved Geranium' (3), Pelargonium peltatum, are good value when considering a collection of indoor garden plants. Both appreciate plenty of water and regular feeding in summer.

Punica granatum 'Nana'

The Pomegranate grows happily in the same situation as the 'Dwarf Orange', but rarely reaches more than 24 inches in height. The orange red tubular flowers (4) are followed by the characteristic fruit which are a slightly paler colour. In winter a minimum of 45 degrees F with only enough water to prevent the soil drying out will be suitable. In summer water and spray the foliage over frequently, and give a liquid feed every 14 days. Re-pot in early spring and prune back any overgrown shoots at the same time.

1

2

3

4

1

2

3

Plumbago capensis

Needs just enough care in cultivation to keep the gardener from becoming complacent.

Good light with full ventilation in summer and freedom from frost in winter are the main demands this plant makes. The blue flowers (1) open at intervals from May–September if the plant is well watered and a liquid feed every 10 days. Prune back the long shoots in winter by up to a half their length. Re-pot during March into any good proprietory compost. Cuttings of side shoots will root if taken in early summer.

Primula

In addition to the Primrose, included in the easy to grow section, there are other Primula well worth including in a list of plants for growing in cool conditions. The popular Pacific hybrid strain of Polyanthus are easily raised from seed and make welcome colour in later winter. They carry their flowers on long stems well above the leaves (2), the colours varying from yellow, blue to cherry red.

Primula x kewensis

This is even easier to grow than Primrose or Polyanthus but is restricted to bright yellow flowers carried on tall elegant stems. I have had plants put up with 38 degrees F for a fortnight at a time, so it will survive in a frost free unheated room.

Primula malacoides

These flower earlier in the year than Kewensis and the range of colour is as diverse as those of the Polyanthus. The candelabra like arrangement of flowers at different levels on the stem gives them a well furnished appearance. Seed is the best method of raising fresh stocks of plants.

Zantedeschia

Until I was presented with the 'Golden Calla', Z. elliottiana to me all Arums were white and only used for funeral decoration. The 'Golden Calla' has large heart shaped leaves, curiously flecked with transparent spots. The flower spathe which grows in late spring, early summer is a good rich yellow (3). They require plenty of water in the growing period, but should be kept fairly dry when resting as the leaves die down. Pot up each year in a peat based compost and increase stock at the same time by removing offsets. A group of the 'Golden Calla' in a bed of ferns shows the quality of flower to good effect.

COOL WITH LIGHT SHADE

Not all plants which will grow in cool conditions prefer full light. Those which in their natural habitat would be found in a woodland situation are best accommodated in a north or west facing room. Included in the group are two shrubs, Hydrangea and Camellia which when they grow large can be planted outdoors.

Camellia

Camellia (1) varieties make large shrubs when planted outdoors but because they flower when quite small – 12 inches or even less – they make useful pot plants. They prefer a semi-shade position and can be stood outdoors for the summer in a sheltered corner. They must never be allowed to dry out at the roots, so water regularly with lime-free water and liquid feed during the growing season. A minimum of 40 degrees F in winter is best, for though they are not permanently harmed by lower temperatures it may inhibit flowering. Re-pot every other year in a lime-free compost. Cuttings of semi-ripened non-flowering side shoots will root well if kept in a propagating case.

Dionaea muscipula 'Venus Fly Trap'

The leaves are edged with stiff hairs (2) so that as they close, any insect which lands on the surface is securely held. The unfortunate prisoner is then dissolved by chemicals exuded from the glands on the leaf and absorbed as food. A compost of peat and sphagnum moss is the mixture I used, and the pot is kept standing on a saucer filled with water. Propagate by division in spring when re-potting.

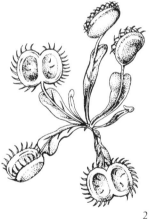

Hydrangea

A semi-shady, well ventilated, cool room from autumn to late spring then a sheltered place outdoors is ideal. Water heavily and feed every 10 days while they are growing, but keep on the dry side during the resting period. Cut back the old flower stems as the colour fades, and re-pot each year in a peat based compost to which has been added aluminium sulphate or a proprietory colourant if you want the flowers to be blue. Cuttings of young shoots can be rooted with fair success. Older plants (3) which are growing in tubs or similar large containers need not be re-potted each year like the young plants. Instead, carefully remove the loose compost and top dress with a fresh mixture with extra fertilizer added. By thinning out the flowering shoots as they develop, those which are left produce much larger flowers.

1

Rhododendron simsii 'Azalea'

A light airy cool position, but shaded from direct sunlight is most suitable. Make certain the root ball is kept moist with tepid lime free or rain water, for hard water will kill them. Stand outside during the summer in a shady place – bury the pot in moist peat, water regularly and liquid feed every 10 days. Bring the Azalea (1) back indoors in late September for flowering in mid winter again. Re-pot in April, in a lime free compost – the proprietory Ericacious mixture is suitable. One of the major problems is to maintain a sufficiently humid atmosphere in average house conditions to prevent the foliage turning brown and the flowers dropping. A plant trough where several plants can be grown together packed round with moist sphagnum moss or similar material helps to solve the dry air problem. Yellow foliage is usually an indication that there is lime in the compost; correct by applying a fertilizer containing soluble iron.

2

Solanum capsicastrum 'Christmas Cherry'

The 'Christmas Cherry' has dark coloured evergreen leaves and can be kept neat by pruning hard in early March, just before re-potting in a peat based compost. Stand the plants outdoors in a frame during May, then as the white flowers open spray them over daily to make certain the berries set. Water heavily in summer and liquid feed every ten days. A cool, partially shaded position is quite suitable once the berries have turned the bright vivid orange. New plants are more easily raised from seed than by means of cuttings. When growing plants from seed a certain amount of 'finger' pruning is essential to promote a good bushy shape. Pinch out the growing tip to make the side growths break (2). Then, in turn when these are long enough nip them back to help flower formation. As the berries swell, move them into good light for ripening, or the plant may shed all or part of the crop.

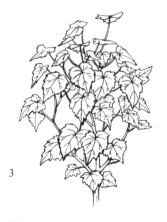

3

Sparmannia africana 'German House Lime'

The 'German House Lime' (3) is certainly more widely grown on the continent than in this country. Though I have grown specimens in pots up to 4 or 5 feet high, 3 feet is about the average. The large grey, green leaves are soft, almost furry to the touch. Clusters of white flowers with protruding yellow tipped red stamens open in winter and spring. Give lots of water in summer, only moderate amounts in winter. Minimum temperature 45 degrees F. Liquid feed from April – September every 14 days. Cuttings taken during May – June are the easiest means of propagation.

WARM WITH LIGHT SHADE

When a higher minimum temperature can be maintained the choice of plants becomes wider. An essential to success is to achieve a high temperature without the air becoming excessively dry. The ideal conditions would be those which prevail in a tropical jungle, impossible on a room scale but practical in the small area occupied by the plants. Grow them packed in peat kept permanently moist.

Ananas comosus 'Variegatus' 'Variegated Pineapple'

'Variegated Pineapple' has creamy white stripes down the leaf margins and the base of the leaves are frequently stained pink which is an attractive variation. They need good light with a little shade in mid-summer and a temperature of not less than 55 degrees F in winter. Pineapples need plenty of water all the year round, although rather less in winter than during a hot summer. A liquid fertilizer applied every 2–3 weeks will promote strong growth. The average time a pineapple takes to reach flowering size is 3 years (1). The parent plant dies, but then suckers grow out at the base which when large enough may be removed and potted up in a loam based compost.

Coleus blumei 'Flame Nettle'

This needs good light or the brightness of the colour contrast in the variegated leaves (2) is lost. Water frequently during the summer but keep the soil only just moist in winter. Apply a liquid feed at 10–14 day intervals from May–August. Pinch back any long shoots to keep the plant in shape. Favourite varieties may be propagated by means of cuttings taken during the summer. Because Coleus are grown for the beauty of leaf only, I remove the flower spikes immediately I notice them.

Cordyline terminalis 'Cabbage Palm'

The 'Cabbage Palm' makes a handsome house plant (3), but unless suitable conditions are provided it promptly dies. Those with cream on red variegated leaves are the most difficult to grow. All need good light and a minimum of 65 degrees F with ample water in the summer and only moderate amounts from October to April. Feed from late April–September and re-pot in a peat based compost every 2 years preferably in spring. Propagation is accomplished by pulling off the suckering shoots which break from the base. Always use soft water – preferably rain-water – and allow the compost to dry on the top between waterings.

Impatiens wallerana 'Holstii' 'Busy Lizzie'

Well grown specimens produce flowers in quantity over a long period in various shades of red and pink and there is even a white petalled variety. During the summer Impatiens need a lot of watering, sometimes every day or even twice a day in hot weather. In winter maintain a temperature above 50 degrees F and keep the compost moist but not saturated. Feed during the summer at 10 day intervals and give shade from very hot sunshine. Re-pot each April using a peat based compost. Cuttings of young shoots should root when placed in a glass of water (1).

Pachystachys lutea 'Lollipop Plant'

In maturity it reaches some 18–20 inches. The bright green leaves are in themselves quietly pleasant, but it is when topped by the bright yellow closely overlapping bracts which hide the flowers that the plant becomes most decorative. The yellow spikes like upside down ice cream cones develop through summer and autumn. Stand in good light but not full sun with a winter minimum temperature of 60 degrees F. Water heavily with soft water in summer and spray over with tepid water occasionally until the spike like bracts show. Cut old plants back and make cuttings of the young shoots which appear. Re-pot each April in a John Innes No 2 compost.

Rechsteineria cardinalis 'Cardinal Flower'

This tuberous rooted perennial from southern America needs a good, well lit draught free place to succeed. The leaves are fairly large (2), soft and velvety to the touch. In the summer bright scarlet flowers on 18 inch stems appear above them. Give the roots ample water in the period May to September, with a liquid feed every ten days. In winter allow it to rest without the water as the foliage dies down. Keep the winter temperature above 55 degrees F. Re-pot each spring preferably into a loam based compost and start watering. Propagate by means of cuttings made from young shoots.

Rhoeo spathacea 'Moses in a Cradle'

Has spear shaped, thickened leaves which are green above and stained purple underneath. They grow in tufted rosettes from a thickened stem (3). Give the plant adequate water in summer with a liquid feed added once every three weeks. Reduce the water supply from September so the compost is almost dry in winter. Re-pot in spring using a peat based compost. Propagate from young shoots which form round the base of the parent plant.

GOOD INDIRECT LIGHT

So many house plants are happier in good but indirect light, and in such conditions some of the most choice foliage plants are worth trying. The value of attractive foliage lies in the fact that it is perennial, whereas flowers are of only short term interest as they quickly fade.

Aglaonema 'Silver Queen'

The leaves are irregularly marbled with various shades of green and silver (1). In winter not less than 55 degrees F is essential with some shade from direct sunlight. Plunge the pot in peat or moist pebbles if the atmosphere is very dry. Water heavily in summer but keep just moist in winter. Feed at 2 week intervals from May–September. Re-pot each spring using a peat based compost.

1

Aphelandra squarrosa 'Louisae' 'Zebra Plant'

The 'Zebra Plant' has large white veined leaved and stiffly erect cockades of yellow flowers (2) in late spring or summer. The spike of flowers should be cut away as the petals fade. Keep the pot standing on a tray of moist pebbles or plunged in peat. They need plenty of water in summer plus a spray over in dry weather, and a liquid feed every 3 weeks. In winter just enough water to prevent the soil drying out. Re-pot in April using a good proprietory compost. Propagate from cuttings taken in summer then rooted in a peat, sand compost over bottom heat.

Begonia rex

Lovely multi-coloured leaves – silver, pink, purple and red (3) are the reward for those who grow this Begonia. Supply a humid atmosphere with liberal watering from May–September plus a liquid feed every 21 days. In winter keep the compost only slightly moist. Re-pot each year during March into a peat compost. Propagate by division or leaf cuttings. A winter temperature of no less than 55 degrees F will be quite suitable.

2

Begonia semperflorens

This is just one of the many beautiful species which make admirable house plants. There are numerous varieties with flowers from white through pink to shades of red. Keep well watered and in a humid climate during summer, with a liquid feed every 10 days. Reduce the water supply in winter and keep the temperature above 50 degrees F. New stock can be raised from seed or by means of cuttings.

3

1

2

3

Beloperone guttata 'Shrimp Plant'

The pinkish, orange bracts which surround the flowers are in evidence for several months which makes the 'Shrimp Plant' (1) good value. Water regularly and feed at 3 week intervals during summer, but in winter water only enough to prevent the compost drying out and keep in a room above 55 degrees F. Cut the top growth back hard before re-potting in April. Cuttings of young shoots offer a ready means of propagation in the springtime.

Codiaeum variegatum 'Pictum' 'Joseph's Coat'

These share a greenhouse with the Orchids which gives some idea of the conditions it needs. Good but indirect light and a humid atmosphere, with a temperature in winter of not less than 60 degrees F. The laurel-like leaves (2) are variously shaded green, pink, scarlet and orange. Water freely in summer and feed once a fortnight, in winter they require just enough moisture to keep the leaves fresh. In April re-pot into a peat based mixture.

Though beautiful, the 'Crotons' are not easy to grow, but so alluring are the different sorts of leaf shape and colour it is worth taking trouble over their cultivation. Cuttings made of young shoots are best taken during the early summer when growth is most vigorous. Rooting is quicker then because it is a simple matter to keep up a high temperature. Make the cuttings fairly long. Dip the tip in rooting powder then insert in a compost of 2 parts peat, 1 sand.

One problem which frequently arises in house culture – the lower leaves turn brown. This may be caused by dryness at the root or in the atmosphere – a condition which is fairly easily corrected.

Dracaena deremensis 'Variegated Dragon Tree'

There are several attractive forms of this deservedly popular foliage plant (3). Which one you choose depends on what colour you prefer. They do need care in watering and just where they are situated in the room. Avoid draughts and make certain the compost is open enough so that excess water drains quickly away. I use a pot with extra large drainage holes as insurance. Keep away from direct sunlight with plenty of water from May to early September and feed every 14 days. In winter maintain a temperature above 60 degrees F and water sparingly. Re-pot in April into a peat based mixture. Sections of stem cut into inch long pieces will root in a heated frame. My own choice of variety would be one known as 'Bausei', with sword like leaves attractively marked with gold.

Fuchsia

No house plant collection is really complete without at least one of the many lovely varieties of Fuchsia (1) which are now obtainable. The main problem is how to prevent flower drop – this is best achieved by standing the pots on a tray of moist pebbles for the summer. Water and spray the foliage, and feed regularly from May to September. In winter keep the soil just moist and the temperature above 50 degrees. Prune top growth back as necessary in February and re-pot into any good proprietory compost. Cuttings taken in April–May root readily enough. Shoots of young growth 3–4 inches long are the best, and sand makes a good rooting medium.

Growing plants from cuttings allows room for experiment in training them into pyramids, standards, and any other shape which the gardener's fancy dictates. By simply removing the tips, a rather leggy, badly furnished cutting can be turned into a neat symmetrical bush.

1

Maranta leuconeura 'Kerchoveana'

Best known as the 'Prayer Plant' (2) because the grey green brown flecked leaves turn up like praying hands at night. This is a beautiful but not easy to grow house plant but the effort to cultivate it is well worth while. Winter is the critical period when the temperature should not be allowed to fall below 60 degrees F. In summer increase the water supply and spray over the leaves with rain water. Feed at fortnightly intervals from May to September. Re-pot every second year into any of the proprietory composts on sale. If fresh stock is required, divide the plants when re-potting. The divisions do not make a great deal of root quickly, so until they establish stand the pots on a gravel tray, if possible with a cover of glass or polythene to keep the atmosphere humid. Moist air and an even temperature are essential if the 'Prayer Plant' is to survive indoors, so even established plants are happier standing on a gravel tray or with the pots plunged in moist peat.

2

Peperomia caperata 'Emerald Ripple'

The 'Emerald Ripple' has deeply ridged leaves, dark green overlaid with flecks of silver (3). The white 'Rats Tail' flowers open during the summer and are not really elegant. Partial shade gives best results with moderate amounts of water in summer and a liquid feed every three weeks. Reduce the watering in winter but maintain a temperature of 50 degrees F. Re-pot each year in spring into any good proprietory compost. Cuttings of mature leaves detached in June–July will root in moist sand and peat.

3

1

2

3

Pteris cretica 'Ribbon Fern'

'Ribbon Fern' is an elegant, graceful fern with deeply divided fronds (1) which make it ideal for a foliage contrast amongst other more ponderous house plants. Like most ferns it enjoys cool humid conditions, so stand the pot on a tray of moist pebbles in a shady corner. Water regularly during the period March to September with a liquid feed added every two weeks. Reduce watering by about three quarters for the winter months. Re-pot each year during April when overgrown plants may be propagated by division.

Saintpaulia ionanthe 'African Violets'

The 'African Violet' is one of these lovely but exasperating plants which is governed by no set of rules.

Well grown plants display bouquets of long lasting flowers which depending on variety can be in shades of deep violet, pink, purple or white. Warmth, moisture and a humid atmosphere are the three main requirements which makes the bathroom a most likely place to grow 'African Violets' in. Water by plunging the pot in a bowl of tepid water, then allowing the surplus water to drain away. Liquid feed every three weeks avoiding at all times wetting the foliage. Keep the plants in good but not direct light with the temperature above 60 degrees F all the year round. Re-pot in the spring using a peat based compost. Leaf cuttings will develop roots if placed in a glass of water, or a sand and peat compost. I prefer to root the leaf cuttings in a 2 parts sand, 1 part peat mixture (2), then there are no problems when the young plantlets are transferred to a growing on compost. Leaf cuttings produce clusters of crowns which make much better flowering plants if teased out and potted up in thumb pots individually. Never put Saintpaulia into over large pots or the compost turns sour and the roots are killed.

Sinningia speciosa 'Gloxinia'

The large flowers, in shape reminiscent of the trumpet of a gramophone (3) can be obtained in a wide variety of colours from violet through crimson, pink and white. Keep the soil well watered while growth is active – March to October, and liquid feed every 10 days until the flower buds show colour. Once flowering is finished gradually reduce the watering until the leaves die. The tuber is then stored in the dry soil away from frost. Re-pot into a standard proprietory compost in February and start the tuber into growth by giving a light spray with tepid water. Propagate by means of seed or leaf cuttings taken during mid-summer.

Smithiantha zebrina hybrids

This Mexican plant which has hairy, begonia like leaves and orange yellow tubular flowers, split at the end intò reflexing segments (1). The flowering season is from June to October. A position in good light, not direct sunlight, with a minimum temperature of 55 degrees F is ideal. They need plenty of water in summer but none at all in winter when the foliage should be allowed to die off leaving only the ruberous root for storing. In March re-pot the tubers into a peat based compost, and spray over every day until growth starts, then water the compost. Start liquid feeding 6 weeks after potting.

Spathiphyllum wallisii

They are like a miniature Arum Lily (2) but last a great deal longer, are tolerant of shade so long as the temperature in winter does not fall below 55 degrees F. Provide a humid atmosphere by spraying the leaves overhead, particularly when the buds are being formed, or they may dry up and not open. Keep the soil evenly moist in summer, slightly less so in winter, but maintain a humid atmosphere all the year round. Re-pot each year into John Innes Compost No 2. Propagate by means of seed or division of the roots when re-potting.

Streptocarpus 'Cape Primrose'

In my experience these are easier to grow than Gloxinia and the smaller flowers carried on long stems are charmingly elegant (3). They appreciate a position away from bright sunlight and a humid climate, so keep the pot plunged in peat or stand it on a tray of moist pebbles. 'Cape Primrose' need plenty of water, preferably lime free during the summer. A weak liquid feed at 10 day intervals helps maintain a succession of flowers. Reduce the water during the winter until the compost is just moist. Re-pot each March using a peat based compost. Propagate by means of seed, or leaf cuttings taken in June–July.

Tradescantia fluminensis 'Spiderwort'

The purple tinted stems and green, cream striped leaves make this a most acceptable trailing plant (4), particularly when it is used in a hanging basket or wall bracket. A well lit position but out of direct sun helps the leaves to gain full colour. Water regularly in summer, less often in winter – just sufficient to prevent the soil drying out completely. Feed every two weeks during summer and re-pot each spring into John Innes No 1 potting compost. Cuttings will root readily if taken during the summer.

Bottle and Terrarium Gardens

1

2

Bottle and Terrarium gardens are the two methods I find most suitable for keeping plants healthy with very little labour in a dry atmosphere. A well furnished miniature garden makes an eye catching piece of decoration. Well cleaned chemical acid carboys, bon-bon jars, wine or cider flagons, aquariums, in fact, any container which lets light in and keeps dry air out can be pressed into service as a mini-garden. Whatever the container chosen it must be clean, this applies especially with carboys which have housed chemicals. To be absolutely sure the container is clean, wash it out with a detergent at least three times and then rinse. A word of warning, be very careful when handling glass carboys. I had one burst while I was washing it out in the bath with disastrous effects on the furnishings and my nerves.

The planting area inside the container is made up with first a layer of pebbles or gravel with some lump charcoal added to prevent the compost becoming sour (1). I find the sticks sold at art shops broken into half inch lengths quite suitable when the bonfire fails to provide charcoal ready to hand. After the pebbles and charcoal add the compost which can either be loam or peat based. The depth depends on the size of container, from a 2 inch layer in a bon-bon jar to 6 inches in the large carboy. By using a paper funnel the compost can be passed into the narrow necked containers without sticking to the sides (2). When using a loam based compost be sure it has been sterilized first to kill weeds, pests and diseases which find conditions inside a bottle garden very much to their liking. Equally, of course, make certain the plants chosen are healthy and free from unwelcome guests such as greenfly.

The choice of plants is also important if the garden is to be a self maintained unit for an appreciable length of time. Avoid quick growing plants which will take over all the available space. Experience has taught me that it is a mistake to put flowering plants into a narrow necked container as removing the decaying petals is like fishing for tiddlers through a hole in the ice – most frustrating.

What to plant in a bottle garden depends on the temperature and light it will be standing in, but most important how much space it provides. The plants listed below all enjoy the conditions a bottle garden offers.

Aphelandra squarrosa

Aphelandra squarrosa has dark green, white veined leaves and cone shaped yellow bracts. It requires slight shade and a minimum of 55 degrees F.

Begonia boweri

Has pink flowers in early spring and green leaves margined with brown. Because it only grows 8–10 inches high qualifies for the mini-garden.

Bromeliads

Collective name for a strange and in many instances beautiful race of plants which enjoy the warmth and humidity supplied by a carboy or terrarium. Cryptanthus acaulis (1) – 'Green Earth Star' is compact enough at 3 inches high.

Calathea insignis

In a container it will only grow to 8–10 inches. The spear shaped leaves (2) are two shades of green on one side and an attractive shade of purple on the reverse. Some shade and a temperature of 55 degrees F.

Calathea makoyana 'Peacock Plant'

The glaucous green rounded leaves are flecked with olive green along the main veins. It needs shade and a temperature of 55 degrees F.

Ficus radicans variegata

One of the smallest variegated forms of the 'Rubber Plant' family, this has attractive silver and green leaves which are carried on stiff stems. Because it is a relatively difficult plant to grow it does do particularly well in the greenhouse-like conditions that a bottle garden offers.

Fittonia argyroneura

Not easy as a normal house plant but grows well in a mini-garden. It gets the popular name of 'Silver Net' because all the leaf veins are picked out in silver (3). Some shade and a minimum temperature of 60 degrees F.

Hedera helix

Any of the small leaved ivys can be accommodated in a cool, partially shaded carboy or terrarium. 'Little Eva' or 'Ivalace' are only two of several suitable varieties.

Maranta leuconeura 'Kerchoveana'

The 'Prayer Plant' is almost my favourite bottle garden plant, the pale green, brown flecked leaves are beautiful. Partial shade and a minimum temperature of 60 degrees F are essential growing conditions.

1

Nertera depressa

'Bead Plant' makes a low hummock of green vegetation, dotted during May with small white flowers which in due course ripen to orange red berries. Partial shade and a minimum temperature of 45 degrees F.

Peperomia caperata 'Emerald Ripple'

The heart shaped leaves develop their lovely silvered sheen (1) in the enclosed shelter of the terrarium. Partial shade and a minimum temperature of 65 degrees F.

Pilea muscosa 'Artillery Plant'

A hummock forming plant growing a tightly interlacing mat of light green foliage (2) up to 9 inches high. Good light and a minimum temperature of 45 degrees F.

Saintpaulia ionanthe 'African Violet'

Because they flower so well 'African Violets' are best grown in a terrarium where the close humid conditions are ideal. The purple, pink, red or white flowers above the soft textured leaves are exhibited over many weeks. Partial shade and a minimum temperature of 60 degrees F.

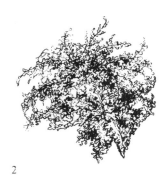

2

Saxifraga sarmentosa

This individual grows so well almost anywhere it is hardly worth space in a mini-garden. However, as it looks pleasant enough grown with small leaved ivy in a cool shady position, there is reason enough to include it. The dark green leaves are heavily veined with white and in spring there are small white flowers.

Selaginella kraussiana

'Creeping Club Moss' (3) is useful as a green carpeting plant. As the name implies, in appearance it is like a hard fronded moss up to 6 inches high. Some shade and a minimum temperature of 50 degrees F suit this plant.

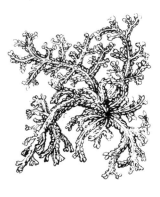

3

Stromanthe amabilis

This requires warm, shaded conditions and so is ideal for the larger bottle garden. Plants really do well in a peaty well aerated compost. Cuttings can be taken at almost any time of the year and should be rooted in fresh clean, moist peat. Check to make sure there are no signs of rotting or dead leaves. I place several cuttings in one pot and that way an early display is assured.

Ferns

Adiantum capillus-veneris 'Maidenhair'
Always looks attractive, the foot long, black stems show the triangular, pale green delicate fronds to good effect. Should be kept cool and shady as harsh light burns the foliage.

Adiantum hispidulum
A most delicate, tropical 'Maidenhair' which grows arching fronds (1) furnished with leaflets that are waved along the top edge. In a bottle garden they can reach 10 inches in height. They require shade and a minimum temperature of 60 degrees F.

1

Pellaea rotundifolia 'Button Fern'
The 'Button Fern' (2) is an interesting arrangement of brown stems and rounded leaflets up to 12 inches high. It needs a good light and a minimum temperature of 50 degrees F.

Phyllitis
There are forms of the 'Harts' Tongue Fern' (3) which add unusual foliage shapes to the container garden. The typical one is long, strap like, but there seems to be infinite variation on this theme. 'Crispum' as the name implies has a crinkled leaf margin, while 'Undulatum' looks as if it has been crimped with curling irons. Both are small enough to be included in a bottle garden or terrarium.

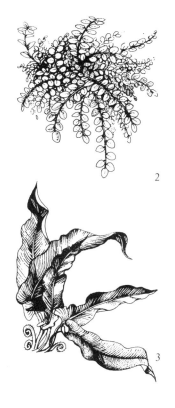

2

One of the lovliest terrarium gardens I ever made was largely composed of native ferns which were presented to me when a friend broke up his collection. The 'Parsley Fern', Cryptogramma crispa as the name implies has tufted fronds growing 8 inches or thereabouts high.

The minute 'Spleenworts', Asplenium are very effective when grown on pieces of limestone placed in a bottle or terrarium. The wall Rue is only 2–3 inches in height, and I first establish plants on a piece of old mortar then transfer the whole lot into the container. A. viride with deeply divided fronds rising from a central rosette is also suitable. Do not make up a container of native ferns by looting the countryside. There are firms who specialise and it is far more fun making a selection with experts to help than by depleting our already threatened wild plants.

3

These are just some of the ferns which I have found very good, though my experiments in this direction have been limited and there must be many more. Most ferns enjoy the cool, humid, cave-like conditions found in a bottle or terrarium garden.

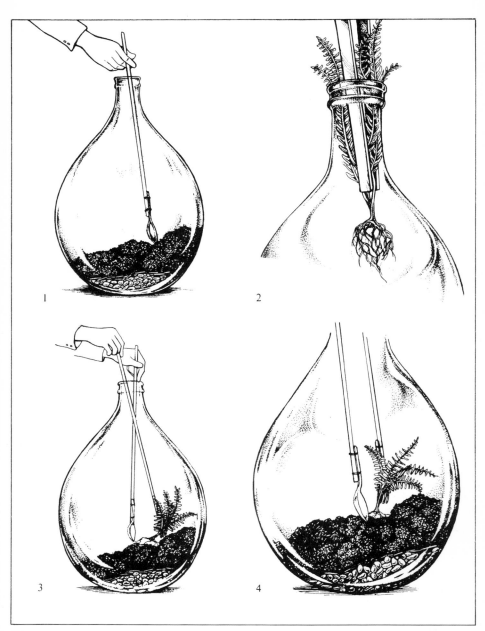

Construction

Having chosen the plants which suit the conditions provided, the way each one is placed in the container is important. Site each so that all its qualities of leaf and flower are seen to best effect. Once the design is decided comes the planting operation. My tools are inexpensive – a dessert spoon (1) and a table fork fastened to bamboo canes. A pair of tweezers made from two flat pieces of ply wood is ideal for inserting ornamental pieces of sculptured stone or cork bark to make a change in level. Each plant can be wrapped in stiff paper as a protection before pushing it through the narrow neck of the carboy or bottle (2). Use the spoon to dig the hole, then with the fork, manoeuvre the plant roots into position (3) and cover them with soil (4). Firming the soil down is not important. Growing conditions in the container are so good the roots soon take hold. When planting is completed, water the compost until it is all thoroughly moist without being waterlogged. I leave the cap, cork or lid off the container for 10 days until it is obvious the compost, plants and watering are in balance, then seal it. No more water should be required for a month or six weeks. After care consists of watering as necessary, pruning excess growth with a razor blade lashed to a cane, and removing dead flowers.

The plants which can be grown in a carboy or bottle show an enormous variation in leaf shape, flower and colour. Containers which can be used as 'grow jars' show almost as wide a selection. Kilner jars, bon-bon jars, a Victorian dome which may have housed a stuffed owl, and only recently an antique olive jar was pressed into service. For flowering plants which need regular attention such as the removal of dead petals I prefer the wide necked jars, otherwise a lot of the pleasure is destroyed. The old fashioned bon-bon jar that was such a feature in the village shop of my childhood make excellent gardens. They can be stood on end with one specimen fern or similar plant of strong character growing in them. Alternatively, when laid on their sides and planted with low growing Saintpaulia or Bromeliads they make very good window decorations in north or west facing rooms. In a typical bottle garden make sure that the tallest plants are in the centre of the design and you should always work from the sides of the bottle inwards. This helps to keep the sides of the bottle clean and the centre plants do not get in the way when planting up the sides. Once you begin to think 'bottle gardening', anything from a brandy glass to the discarded flask from a chemistry set becomes material for experimenting with. Acquire the container, then choose plants to fit it.

Terrarium

A plant case or terrarium is much easier to look after and the whole top cover can be removed when any of the occupants need attention. I much prefer a terrarium as a mini-garden. It allows so much more room for landscape and plant grouping, and with the help of some stones and pieces of wood you can create a mini-woodland scene.

All the plants appropriate for a carboy or bottle garden can be grown in a terrarium, plus almost the whole range of house plants as well. Only the limits of plant size and available space impose any restrictions on the terrarium gardener. Feeding of plants in a bottle or terrarium garden is, I feel, a mistake. It just encourages them to outgrow the space. Instead, when one of the original plants grows too large and pruning is not practicable, simply lift it out, add a little fresh compost and plant something smaller, preferably a rooted cuttings taken from the offending specimen.

When arranging the plants do make sure that the tallest are placed at the back of the terrarium garden and the smaller ones at the front. Think about the location of the unit in the room and remember never to place it in full sun. Direct sun through a glass container can wreak havoc with delicate foliage. As an extra incentive, the most attractive indoor garden I ever made was in an old aquarium which was no longer sufficiently watertight to serve as a fish tank, but which made a superb terrarium.

The principle of the terrarium or bottle garden is simply that of a self contained, virtually self perpetuating unit. Water is taken from the compost with nutrients dissolved in it through the plant roots and passed up to the leaves. During daylight hours, of course, the normal process of food manufacturing takes place in the foliage. Surplus moisture passes out through the leaves – the moisture runs down the sides of the container to be taken up by the roots once more. Included in the process are the production of and use of carbon dioxide and oxygen in just about equal proportions, so the balance inside the jar is constant. Plants growing in a properly balanced community as described need practically no attention for anything up to 6 months, presenting the nearest thing to perpetual motion which the gardener is likely to encounter. There are on the market beautiful reproductions of Victorian terrariums for use both inside the house, or as in one flat I visited recently a glass covered window box. An old brandy glass is another useful object which can be pressed into service as a container. It is particularly useful when growing dwarf cacti and succulents. As the greenhouse is to the garden in protecting plants from the cold, so is the terrarium indoors shielding plants from hot, dry air.

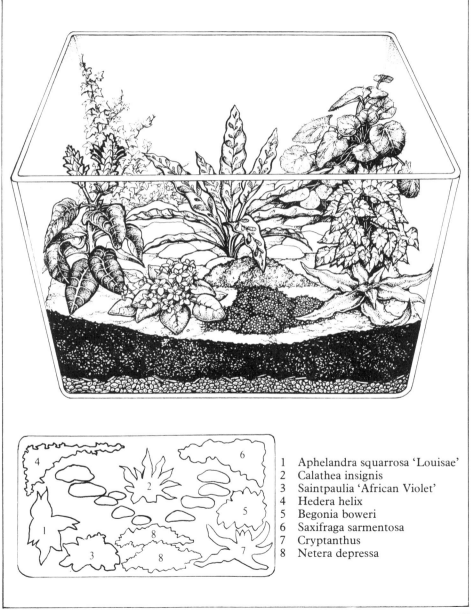

1 Aphelandra squarrosa 'Louisae'
2 Calathea insignis
3 Saintpaulia 'African Violet'
4 Hedera helix
5 Begonia boweri
6 Saxifraga sarmentosa
7 Cryptanthus
8 Netera depressa

Plants from seed

The childhood habit of sowing pips from grapefruit or saving the top from a pineapple just to see if it can be persuaded to root in a prepared compost is carried on by gardeners into adult life.

Germinating the harder coated seed is the first problem to overcome and this is really not difficult to accomplish, for on reflection plants sow seed every year with no help at all from the gardener. The seed which needed the most persuasion to germinate when I first tried sowing it was the Date Palm. Experiments using water, moist compost, rolling the stones in wet felt have all been discarded in favour of shaking the stones up in moist peat inside a polythene bag, then hanging them up in the airing cupboard. Use the stones from the freshest dates, the peat should be just wet enough – when squeezed the water eases out between the fingers. In a month to six weeks a shoot like a grass sprout appears and the stone may then be potted up into a peat based mixture and brought into the light. Keep the palm well watered in a warm humid room, free from draughts and it makes an uncommon house plant.

Avocado pear are often grown from seed, and for a time until they outgrow the house do make a noteworthy pot plant. The stone can be started into growth either by burying a third of its depth in moist compost or by the more curious method of suspending it in water (1). Whichever way is used roots develop quicker if the stone is wounded by nicking it with a sharp knife or by inserting a piece of string or a matchstick through the base (2). Once the roots show pot the stone up in John Innes No 1 compost or a peat based mixture. In summer germination takes about 5 weeks, other times about 8. Once started, growth is so quick it may have to be potted on into a larger container twice a year.

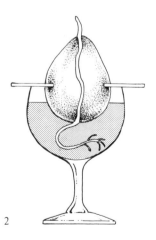

The 'pips' of citrus fruits – lemon, orange and grapefruit – are all easy to germinate. Sow the seeds in a shallow tray or half pot filled with peat based compost, cover with a polythene bag and stand them in the airing cupboard. Within about 4 weeks the shoots will be showing and the container needs to be moved into full light. The seedlings should be potted into individual containers when they are 4 inches high. A liquid feed every 2 weeks will help to keep the leaves a shiny healthy green, especially if a pinch of magnesium sulphate (Epsom salts) is added twice a year: in April and again in June. By careful pruning the tiny citrus bushes can be kept to shape. When this is done depends on flowering and fruiting, but I prefer to do any thinning with a pair of sharp scissors in May. Citrus need full sun all the year round.

Though fresh pineapple is not commonly served as dessert, at least not to the same extent as apples or pears, they do feature occasionally. Instead of throwing the top out for compost, cut it off together with about an inch of skin and pot it up in a sandy compost (1). Topped up with about half an inch of sharp, lime free sand. To assist with rooting, slip the pot inside a polythene bag, and stand it in a warm place (2). When rooted pot the new plant up in a proprietory compost (3). Pineapples need high humidity and at least 60 degrees F, though even then they are unlikely to fruit unless kept in a hot house. The one occasion when a pineapple consented to fruit for me was during the burning hot summer of 1976. Having endured the comments visitors make about the rather ugly looking, heavily barbed leaves amongst the conventional pot plants, I lavished all my care on persuading it to fruit. Potted in a rich compost with regular liquid feeding the plant did, indeed fruit, and even greater triumph the flavour was superb. All the enthusiast requires is optimism, a pineapple crown and another summer like 1976. There is special pleasure in fruiting a really exotic edible plant.

1

There are many fruit trees which can be grown from seed and when large enough planted outdoors. Unfortunately, there is no guarantee of the quality of the fruit when they do come into bearing. This should not deprive the indoor gardener of the pleasure of sowing the stones from a succulent peach, juicy plum or crisp apple.

2

Large stones like those of the peach, almond and apricot should be planted one to a pot. Small pips of apple or pear are sown 4 or 5 to a pot, then moved into individual containers when large enough to handle. Several of the most popular apple and pear varieties were raised by pip sowing amateurs, so to the pleasure of growing things from seed is added the excitement of raising a new variety to surpass even Cox's Orange Pippin for flavour. Hard stones such as peach need the shell weakening by either filing or just cracking it slightly with a hammer, or they take months to germinate.

Coffee plants enjoyed a sudden burst of popularity when 'do it yourself' enthusiasts decided to grow their own beans for grinding. In fact, coffee beans will germinate quite quickly in a moist warm compost. The resulting shrub has attractive shiny dark evergreen foliage which, even lacking the incentive of free coffee still makes a quietly pleasing house plant.

3

Lychees, peanuts, horsechestnuts, indeed anything which has either interesting foliage, flowers or commercial potential can be grown from seed. Just placing an orange pip into soil and watching it grow may start a child on a life long hobby.

Herbs

Chives (1) are not hard to grow in a pot on a sunny windowsill. Sow the seeds or, if available, pot up the roots in loam based compost. Keep them well watered and liquid feed as the roots fill the pot. The purple flowers which open in June are an additional bonus. Divide and re-pot each spring. The pot can stand outside in summer.

Mint grows to about 18–24 inches high in a pot, but being hardy can stand outdoors on a balcony or windowsill from April onwards. Pot the roots up in February into a six inch pot or similar sized container. Once growth starts keep well watered and feed every 10 days. Pick the shoots when they are 3–4 inches tall.

Marjoram ('**Sweet**') (2) is so pleasantly fragrant it is worth growing for that reason alone. In maturity the reed-like stems carry pink flowers. Sow seeds of 'Sweet Marjoram' which is the most popular variety during March into a standard compost. When large enough pot up the seedlings into 3 inch pots and stand them on a light windowsill. The stems can be cut when about 6 inches tall.

Parsley makes a good house plant as the curling moss like leaves are pleasant to look at. When there is room for only one herb, this is the most useful. Sow seeds in any standard compost during March, and pour a kettle of boiling water over them to quicken germination. To keep up a succession of young plants make further sowings at intervals during the year. Pot the seedlings on into 4 inch pots, keeping them well watered. Pick the shoots regularly so the plant bushes out, otherwise the leaves become coarse.

Sage (3) One of the popular herbs, sage is an 'evergreen' grey leaved shrub, pleasantly aromatic. Sow the seeds in loam based compost in March. Pot the seedlings on when 2 inches high into 3 inch pots and stand in a sunny window. Keep them well watered, potting on as required into 5 inch pots. Sprigs may be cut for use as flavourings when the shoots are 6–8 inches long.

Thyme (4) There are many different varieties of thyme, but the common Thymus vulgaris is the one most used in cooking. Sow the seed in spring, then prick out the seedlings first into thumb and then into 3 inch pots using a loam based compost. Keep in full sun and water frequently or growth becomes stunted. Sprigs may be cut when shoots are long enough, and the mauve flowers are a bonus in July.

Fruit and Vegetables

Aubergine Egg Plant (1) Sow the seed during March into a peat based compost, then pot on into larger containers when big enough to handle easily. Keep the pot in good light with shade from the hottest sun. Water regularly and liquid feed every ten days. When the plant is 6–8 inches high pinch out the growing tip to encourage side shoots to develop. These side shoots should be limited to 3 or 4 and allowed to bear 1 fruit each. Once the fruit are fully developed pick and use or they lose their flavour.

Courgettes (2) can be cropped in compost filled bags standing on a balcony or roof. Alternatively they can be planted in a window box. A rich fibrous compost is essential so mix in peat or rotted manure with the loam for window box culture. Sow the seed in boxes during late March, then plant out when 3 leaves or more have developed into a pot, bag or box. Keep them well watered and liquid feed every 6 days once the plants are in full growth. Pick the fruit when they are about 5 inches long.

Peppers (3) Providing the plants can be given a south facing window or similar sunny position, peppers are not difficult to grow. Sow the seeds in mid March into 2 inch peat pots. Once the roots are showing through the side and base of the pot, I plant into a 5 inch pot or compost filled polythene bag. Pots are most suitable as they can easily be accommodated on a window sill. For the final potting I use John Innes No 3 potting compost, keep it moist and syringe the leaves over every day, particularly when the flowers are open as it helps the fruit to set. As with tomatoes, once the fruit are visible, a liquid feed every ten days will help them to swell. Pick the peppers while still green.

Lettuce is a top priority crop for those who like fresh salad. To keep up a succession of mature lettuce sow a pinch of seed at 14 day intervals from February until September. In the average household growing lettuce in winter without supplementary lighting is not easy. Once the seed has germinated prick the required number of lettuce off into deep boxes or whatever container is available. Unlike carrots, lettuce are not long rooted so, providing the soil is fertile, they will grow well enough in a shallow container – 4–6 inches in depth. The remaining seedlings can be left to grow on to be used as leaf salads when they are big enough. Lettuce take from 8–13 weeks to reach maturity depending on the time of year. Keep them well watered during the growing season and give a liquid feed 6 weeks after pricking out and thereafter at 10 day

1

2

3

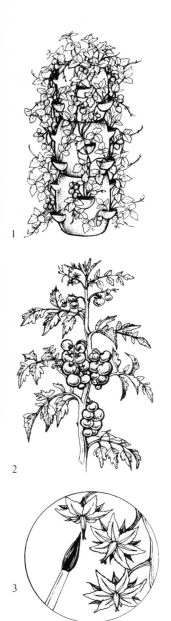

intervals. Dwarf varieties like 'Little Gem' – March to August, 'Tom Thumb – February to April, or 'All the Year Round' are most convenient in limited space.

Runner Beans are only practicable where there is space on a balcony, roof garden or patio for a deep box, tub or growing bag. Sow 2 seeds into a 3 inch pot during late March or April. Then if both germinate, remove the weakest. When large enough, plant up in their cropping position – provided they can be protected from frost. Some support – either netting or canes must be given for the stems to climb up. Keep well watered and commence feeding as the first flower buds show. The variety 'Blue Lake' or 'Sprite' are most suitable for this type of gardening.

Strawberries can be planted up in window boxes, barrels, grow bags or a pyramid of pots (1) which may be bought ready made. Use a good quality proprietory compost – John Innes No 2 or 3 with extra part of peat added. Buy young plants which are guaranteed virus free and plant them in the containers during September. Keep them well watered, then, when the fruit starts to swell apply a liquid feed every 10 days.

Tomatoes (2) are a crop which most people with an interest in gardening try to grow. There is no other crop whose development can be so intimately observed as the tomato. From the moment the seed leaves poke through the compost to the pollinating of the flowers and ripening of the fruit nothing is hidden. Sow the seed in peat or loam based compost in April, keeping the pots in a temperature of 60–65 degrees F. When the young plants are showing the first pair of true leaves pot them into 3 inch peat pots using the standard compost. Grow them on until the first truss of flowers is showing, but before they open plant them in grow bags, 8 inch pots, or whatever container is being used. If possible, in early June, stand the plants outdoors against a sunlit wall. Keep them well watered all the time. Remove side shoots which appear in the leaf axils before they grow too big.

Using a dry piece of cotton wool or a soft camel hair brush (artist's) dust the flowers as they open to fertilize them (3). Shaking the plant is often enough to transfer the pollen, then spray the foliage with clean water – fruit will not set in a dry atmosphere. Once the first truss of fruit is set start applying a liquid feed every 5 days. When the plant has up to 5 trusses of fruit showing nip out the growing tip to prevent any further extension growth. Tomatoes grown like this rarely ripen more than 5 trusses.

Pests

Aphids (greenfly and blackfly) A common pest which feeds on plant sap, distorting young growths and leaving a sticky honeydew on the leaves. They also transmit virus diseases.

Control Wash the plant in soap and water. Spray with liquid derris or a systemic insecticide.

Mealy Bugs Adult females resemble small woodlice covered in a white mealy wax and the eggs look like flecks of cotton wool. The stem and leaves feel sticky, the leaves turn yellow and growth is weakened. Usually found in the leaf axils.

Control Dab the colonies with methylated spirits or spray with systemic insecticide.

Miner (leaf) Larvae make white tunnels inside the leaves – leaves develop brown blotches.

Control Remove badly damaged leaves containing pest. Spray with malathion (Not ferns or succulents).

Red Spider Mite These thrive in a centrally heated atmos-phere. The leaves lose glossy sheen and look grey and the surface becomes flecked with white spots when held up to the light. Growth is restricted.

Control Wash in liquid derris and soft soap. Spray with systemic or malathion.

Scale Leaves and stems covered with small brown lumps which look like immobile tortoises.

Control Rub off with a brush dipped in methylated spirits or spray with systemic insecticide.

Thrip Tiny, black midge like insects whose feeding habits cause leaves to look silvery grey. Buds are distorted and petals flecked with brown.

Control Spray with malathion or systemic immediately damage is noticed.

Whitefly A troublesome pest – clouds of white insects fly up when pot is shaken. Foliage turns pale and the plant can be killed.

Control Spray with malathion or systemic insecticide after washing the plants in soft soap and water.

Vine Weevil Pieces eaten out of foliage – fat white grubs feeding on the roots which eventually kills the plant.

Control Water with systemic insecticide or dust with B.H.C. dust on top of compost.

N.B. Food crops should *not* be eaten within seven days of an application of a systemic insecticide. Wash before eating.

Diseases

Botrytis Shows itself as dusty patches on leaves or stems.

Control Improve ventilation and spray with systemic fungicide. Avoid condensation on leaves; remove dead material.

Crown and Stem Rot Rotting of stem at soil level or young shoots.

Control Reduce the water. Cut away rotting tissue and dust wound with Captan or flowers of sulphur.

Mildew White powder on leaves and flower buds.

Control Improve air circulation. Reduce water supply. Spray with Karathane or systemic fungicide.

Root Rot Plants wilt due to over watering. Roots slimey and rotten and soil smells sour.

Control Re-pot into fresh compost after removing any rotten roots and dusting the remainder with flowers of sulphur or Captan. DO NOT OVER WATER.

Cultural problems (Physiological Disorders)

Brown leaves Leaf drop Usually caused by faulty watering, hot dry air or draughts.

Plant wilts Dryness of the air or at the roots, or over watering.

Leaves feel brittle and leathery This can be caused by an excess of fertilizer, so reduce feeding and thoroughly soak pot in a bowl of soft water.

Yellow Leaves In rhododendrons this may be caused by an iron deficiency. Water with chilated iron.

In citrus it is usually due to magnesium deficiency. Water with Epsom Salts – teaspoonful to a pint of water.

Paling of leaves and spindly growth Usually not enough light, so move to window sill with good light (but not bright sunlight).

Spots on leaves Due to water splashes or sun scorch. Can also be caused by fungal spores.

Check all newly acquired plants carefully for pests or diseases before adding them to the house collection. Prevention is *the* best control.

MAKE sure that all chemicals are used in strict accordance with the manufacturers' instructions.

MAKE a special note which plants should *not* be sprayed with a certain chemical.

MAKE a special note of the time lapse required before eating a treated crop.

Index